ACADEMIC TURNAROUNDS

Restoring Vitality to Challenged American Colleges and Universities

Edited by
Terrence MacTaggart

Library of Congress Cataloging-in-Publication Data

Academic turnarounds : restoring vitality to challenged American colleges and universities / edited by Terrence MacTaggart.
    p. cm. — (ACE/Praeger series on higher education)
Includes index.
ISBN–13: 978–0–275–98806–7 (alk. paper)
ISBN–10: 0–275–98806–6 (alk. paper)
1. Public universities and colleges—United States—Administration. 2. University autonomy—United States. 3. Higher education and state—United States. I. MacTaggart, Terrence J., 1946–
    LB2341.A2295 2007
    378.1'010973   2006039613

British Library Cataloguing in Publication Data is available.

Library of Congress Catalog Card Number: 2006039613
ISBN–13: 978–0–275–98806–7
ISBN–10: 0–275–98806–6

First published in 2007

Praeger Publishers, 88 Post Road West, Westport, CT 06881
An imprint of Greenwood Publishing Group, Inc.
www.praeger.com

Printed in the United States of America

The paper used in this book complies with the Permanent Paper Standard issued by the National Information Standards Organization (Z39.48–1984).

10 9 8 7 6 5 4 3 2 1

ACADEMIC TURNAROUNDS

CONTENTS

SECTION THREE: LESSONS FOR LEADERS

PREFACE

The idea for this book stemmed from my experiences as a member, and chair, of the Commission on Institutions of Higher Education of the New England Association of Colleges and Schools. That is a mouthful to be sure, but it is an important agency, even if little known outside higher education circles. The commission recommends approval, or denial, of accreditation for all the colleges and universities in the six New England states. If a college is denied accreditation, or even if it receives public notice that its accreditation is in doubt, its students lose their access to federal financial aid. Either of those actions would put most colleges out of business.

At regular intervals, each New England institution of higher learning must submit to the commission written evidence of its financial soundness and its educational quality. Then it must send appropriate representatives—usually the president, perhaps accompanied by a chief academic officer, a finance official, and a trustee—to make a case for their institution, and implicitly, for their own effective leadership, before commission members. The result of that review is usually a foregone conclusion. The majority of those reviewed are accredited, or retain their accreditation, that is, preserve their eligibility to enroll students who receive federal financial aid.

In the nine years that I served on the commission, including three as its chair, I found much to admire in the schools that came before the group. However, the most compelling cases were not those reputable, reasonably well-financed, solid places that New England seems to have in good supply. Instead, I found most intriguing those that had slipped, at least toward mediocrity, and perhaps to the brink of extinction, but had somehow found the leadership and imagination to redeem themselves—had become more vital, healthy enterprises.

Those turnaround institutions fell into two groups: those that teetered on the brink of bankruptcy, and those that had drifted downward in quality, reputation, and finances, but were in no immediate danger of extinction. The future of the first group was perennially in doubt. A negative announcement from an accrediting agency, a modest drop in enrollment, a lender's decision to call in a loan—any one of those might mean the institution would go under.

The second group of turnaround institutions had a less severe plight, because their financial bases insulated them from changes in student demand, bad decisions, or inadequate leadership. Those schools also transformed themselves into stronger, more vibrant, and financially secure enterprises. Their leaders heeded the early warning signs of fiscal, reputational, and academic decline and acted in time to revive the institution.

This book focuses on the paths taken by colleges and universities in both categories. All of them became financially secure, respected, and educationally important enterprises.

Why do some schools change course and turn toward prosperity while others languish—if not on the tip of disaster, at least far below their potential for quality and distinction? The answer appears to depend on responses to four sets of questions.

WHAT IS A TRUE TURNAROUND?

What does it mean for an institution to experience a turnaround? How does a true turnaround differ from a successful enrollment management campaign, or a new marketing strategy, or cost cutting that improves the bottom line? What are the differences and similarities between turnarounds in public institutions and their private counterparts?

WHAT ARE THE CRITICAL SUCCESS FACTORS?

Why are some institutions able to transform themselves, while others facing similar challenges at best muddle along, or, at worst, suffer declines in enrollment, finances, reputation, and quality? What are the factors that set successful institutions apart from the also-rans? How can other institutions in distress replicate those factors?

WHAT ARE THE STAGES OF A TURNAROUND?

What are the discrete segments of a turnaround process? Do all successful turnarounds involve the same stages, in the same sequence? What metrics can measure the progress of a turnaround strategy?

WHO LEADS A TURNAROUND?

What kind of leadership is required of turnarounds? Are some leadership styles more useful than others for different stages of the turnaround process? What is the essential role of presidents? trustees? senior officers? faculty? donors? state and federal regulators? accreditors?

To answer those questions in detail required both data and cooperation.

From a list of more than 100 colleges and universities that had reputations for having dramatically improved themselves, some 40 received an in-depth review. Those comprise 31 independent schools and 9 publicly supported colleges, universities, or systems. We discuss an array of institutions, ranging from substantial private research universities such as Syracuse University, the University of Denver, and Northeastern University, to smaller liberal arts colleges such as Green Mountain College and Regis College, to successful liberal arts cum career universities such as Quinnipiac University, to distinctive publics such as the College of New Jersey and the University of Connecticut. (Although community colleges and proprietary schools do turn themselves around, we focus on not-for-profit institutions that offer at least a four-year degree.)

We chose those colleges and universities because they illustrated important features of turnarounds generally and either their administrative leaders granted us full access or their turnaround stories were well known to us, or widely reported. The comprehensive transformations described in this book are more likely to occur at independent rather than public institutions, for reasons advanced in chapter 6. Thus, three-quarters of the cases mentioned are drawn from private higher education. Where our comments might be construed as negative toward a school or its leadership, we do not disclose the names of institutions. But all the comments in the book are based on actual institutional experiences, as we understand them.

Information from a project funded by the Davis Education Foundation was vital to the book. As part of its commitment to sustaining small colleges in New England, in 2004, the foundation funded an effort to enable 33 small private colleges to develop their capacity to use financial indicators. I participated in discussions with executives at approximately a third of those institutions about strategies and management practices they used to strengthen their financial bases.

They shared their experiences willingly, dissected their individual turnaround sagas, and identified turning points and phases of change. Indeed, all those interviewed for this book were remarkably candid about both what worked and what did not.

This book is a result of defining the important questions and then analyzing the answers of those who facilitated successful institutional change. By appreciating the characteristics of successful turnarounds, more leaders, especially presidents and trustees, will be better able to transform America's under-performing and distressed colleges and universities.

INTENDED AUDIENCES

This book is intended as a must-read for leaders at colleges and universities in need of a turnaround. Trustees and presidents in particular should read the entire book. It will help them assess the financial condition of their institution, as well as its prospects. Leaders in doubt—or denial—about what a distressed college or university requires will get the tools for understanding how bad their situation is and what must be done to improve it. Leaders at schools that have begun to rebound will find the descriptions of turnaround stages (chapters 1, 2, 3, and 4) helpful in evaluating their progress and considering their next steps.

Donors, accreditors, and regulators will find this book useful in identifying ways to help troubled schools find a brighter future. Donors, for example, who wish to support strategic change, rather than merely provide a bail out, will find the chapters on financial turnarounds (chapters 1, 2, and 5) especially relevant. State approving authorities and accrediting agencies can look to chapters 2 and 8 to inform their questions about financial and academic vitality at turnaround institutions. Auditors and bond-rating agencies will find useful ideas in this book for assessing the future viability of institutions seeking unqualified opinions and favorable interest rates.

As noted in chapter 2, very often the faculty must lead trustees to see that only new leadership will reverse a downward trajectory. Thus faculty leaders at challenged institutions will find this book instructive as they attempt to diagnose the malaise they perceive, to capture the attention of trustees, and to participate in a turnaround that may save their livelihoods.

STRUCTURE OF THE BOOK

The book is organized into three sections. The first section, "The Natural History of Turnarounds," contains four chapters that detail the three stages common to academic transformations: fiscal reform, matching institutional strengths to market needs through marketing and branding, and a comprehensive change we describe as academic revitalization. The second section focuses on topics of interest to two groups of readers: presidents, financial officers, and trustees with special responsibility for overseeing the fiscal affairs of their institution; and those concerned with the unique features of turnarounds at state-supported colleges and universities. The final section summarizes the lessons to be learned from the turnaround stories. Chapter 7 offers practical advice to new presidents charged with transforming beleaguered schools, and the last chapter advises trustees, donors, and accreditors on their opportunities to have a positive influence on turnarounds.

Chapter 1 presents my analysis of the three overlapping stages in the turnaround process: restoring financial health; marketing programs and branding the revived institution; and redefining the educational mission and culture. The chapter contrasts elements of the stages with a matrix relating those stages to variables that include leadership qualities; the change process itself; modifications in academic programs; time; the role of trustees; external support; and financial indicators.

In chapter 2, I focus on restoring financial health, the first stage required in most, but not all, turnarounds. The chapter draws examples from an institution on the verge of bankruptcy, as well as from two institutions with adequate—but declining—resources. It also identifies five critical success factors that characterize viable financial transformations: engaging new leaders; ensuring accurate financial information; focusing on financial problems, communicating fiscal realities clearly; and engaging faculty in the difficult process of financial improvement.

Jerry Berberet, drawing primarily from the experiences of members of Associated New American Colleges, discusses in chapter 3 the importance of marketing and branding, defining that process as the development and communication of an attractive image that accurately reflects the core values and strengths of a college or university. The author examines such components as the role of recruiting strategies, new curricular emphases, and even physical improvements, in the process of elucidating and disseminating institutional image.

Chapter 4, written by Adrian Tinsley, addresses true academic revitalization. Some institutions cease the turnaround process once they have achieved financial stability and a modest rebranding. Others, however, engage in a more arduous—and much longer—journey, rethinking trenchantly the mission of the institution and all its academic and educational operations. As the chapter notes, real turnarounds are a combination of leadership, inherited culture, governance, location, and other factors unique to each institution. Drawing primarily on the experiences of the University of Denver, the College of New Jersey, and Northeastern University, the chapter describes how those institutions and their leaders have negotiated profound transformation.

In chapter 5, Michael Townsley presents a primer on what turnaround leaders need to know about financial analysis and indicators. The topics include detecting the early warning signs of fiscal distress, selecting and understanding appropriate indicators for each stage in the turnaround, and using financial information to communicate to internal and external audiences. He provides a systematic guide for presidents, financial officers, and trustees who must command the fiscal health of their institutions.

In chapter 6, I outline the realities of bringing about change in the public sector. While state-supported colleges, universities, and systems pursue turnarounds akin to those at independent colleges, they do so in an overtly political environment. I point out that engineering change in the public sector demands recognition of the priority of the public's agenda, the diffusion of authority among many players, the power of legislators to set—and set aside—educational policy, and governance in the sunshine.

In chapter 7, Kenneth Shaw proffers practical advice to a new president with the ambition to take on a transformational role. Shaw figuratively walks that individual through considerations prior to taking the job, as well as tasks before assuming the mantle, and offers sage advice on how to actually accomplish necessary changes.

In the final chapter, I offer straightforward counsel to trustees, donors, and accreditors. The core message is that actions should be thoughtfully tailored to an understanding of a school's stage in its turnaround process. Trustees will alternatively act as the ultimate authority at an institution, as its advocates, and as colleagues, depending on particular turnaround tasks. Donors who really want to help accelerate a turnaround must provide unrestricted cash in the early stages but can tailor gifts to support academic reform in later phases. Finally, accrediting associations will find that the best way to aid distressed institutions is to get tough with them. Few stimulants will encourage trustees to get the right leader and provide the financial support necessary as will the threat to withdraw accreditation and deny the school access to federal financial aid.

ACKNOWLEDGMENTS

This book is better than it might have been thanks to the work of many thoughtful people. The contributing authors, Jerry Berberet, Kenneth Shaw, Adrian Tinsley, and Michael Townsley, added depth that could not have been found from others. As head of the Associated New American Colleges, Jerry Berberet participated in one of the great turnaround dramas in the modern history of American higher education. Kenneth Shaw is widely recognized not only for restoring strength to Syracuse University, one of the nation's finest research institutions, but also for his practical reflections on leadership as an author and mentor. Adrian Tinsley has inspired a generation of leaders through her transformational work at Bridgewater State College and her leadership of the Bryn Mawr Institute for Women in Higher Education. Michael Townsley, the former president of the Pennsylvania Institute of Technology, is a national expert on restoring financial health to small colleges. It is hard to imagine a more suitable array of contributors to a book on this topic.

The book benefited from the skill of two wonderful editors. Susan Slesinger of ACE/Praeger provided timely, correct—and sometimes tart—advice when it was needed most. Anne Ruffner Edwards, who worked with me in Maine, has a background in public policy and a concern for clear, interesting prose, both of which contributed mightily to the readability of this text.

Two experts and friends helped to sharpen the central theses of the book in its early stages. Tom Longin, academic leader at several independent colleges, former vice president of the Association of Governing Boards, and consultant to small- and medium-sized institutions, shaped the ideas on turnaround leadership. Charles Cook, former head of the higher education commission of the New England Accrediting Association and now a senior vice president at Johnson & Wales University, brought his immense experience to bear on most of the assertions in this book.

The presidents, trustees, senior officers, faculty and staff, and others who provided their reflections on the transformation of their institutions were essential to this work. I deeply appreciate their willingness to disclose so much about their strategies, as well as their candor regarding the turnaround process.

Finally, I would like to thank, and acknowledge the support of, the trustees of the University of Maine System. They provided a research professorship that enabled me to do the research and writing for this book and for several other related projects.

SECTION I

The Natural History of Turnarounds

CHAPTER

The Three Stages of College and University Revitalization

Terrence MacTaggart

Turnaround sagas are remarkable in that they are at once unique and yet much alike. Each change story exhibits strikingly particular features of locale, culture, mission, history, leadership temperament, resources, and programs. At the same time, each story displays marked similarities in the sequence and character of the stages of its journey to a more prosperous future. From Green Mountain College, a small environmental cum liberal arts school nestled in the remote Vermont hamlet of Poultney, to the bustling campus of Northeastern University, where more than twenty thousand students learn in the heart of Boston, the turnaround trajectories—but not the details—are much the same.

This chapter describes the three stages in turnarounds that we observed in many institutions. Understanding this progression will enable leaders to pinpoint the position of their institution on the turnaround trajectory; to evaluate how well they are doing at the current point in the turnaround process; and to decide what they need to do next.

THE THREE STAGES

Restoring financial stability is often the first stage in a turnaround. It is *always* a necessary first step for colleges and universities in serious financial distress. Marketing academic programs and branding or rebranding an institutional image typically make up the second stage. A third stage, though one not achieved or even imagined by some institutions, is revitalizing the academic program and the institution's culture.

Stage I: Restoring Financial Stability

Severely distressed institutions facing imminent closure, merger, or sale must restore solvency or accept one of those unattractive destinies. Denial of the problems, and of the consequences of ignoring them, is a surprisingly common habit among trustees and executives alike. At one beleaguered institution that ultimately closed it doors, the trustees came to grips with their responsibilities only after an attorney defined for them the meaning of fiduciary. Such hesitancy only defers the inevitable reckoning and makes a turnaround even more difficult.

Facing a $5 million lawsuit from a contractor, nearly $2 million in overdue debts to local vendors, red ink on the bottom line of the income statement, and a tuition-discount policy that guaranteed increased deficits as enrollments grew, Jack Brennan, the new president at Green Mountain College, knew without question that restoring fiscal health was his first job, or no one at the college would have a job at all.

Jim Greismer faced challenges nearly as desperate when became the chief financial officer at the University of Denver in January 1990. The new president, Dan Ritchie, persuaded Greismer to take the job even though DU had a cumulative deficit of $8 million; an operating shortfall of nearly $1.5 million; a seriously decaying campus infrastructure; and real concern about meeting payroll. Or maybe Greismer came because of the mighty challenges. Whatever the motivation, those two men had to fix the chronic money problems, or the oldest independent university in the Rocky Mountain West might not see the new century.

Even where budgets are balanced and money is in the bank, forecasts of financial stress present early warning signs: prompt action may prevent a future crisis. When Kenneth "Buzz" Shaw came to Syracuse University in 1991, burgeoning enrollments and winning sports teams masked deep fiscal problems. An analysis of the budget, begun under his predecessor, revealed Syracuse's financial vulnerabilities. Shaw realized that without dramatic and difficult program and staff cuts, the fiscal problem would quickly become a crisis.

Financial Turnarounds at Public Colleges and Universities

Public colleges and universities, protestations to legislatures notwithstanding, seldom face the same degree of fiscal distress as their independent peers. ("For the first time in my life, I have to make a payroll," lamented Charles Graham after leaving a regional state institution to take on the presidency of Hamline University, in St. Paul, for example.) Salaries of public college and university employees are relatively secure. But legislators often need to be persuaded that the people's money is being well spent before they will vote for additional funds. Turnarounds at two small public colleges, both located far from the centers of commerce and power in their states, illustrate that point.

The University of Wisconsin in Superior, located in the northeast corner of the state, was the smallest institution in Wisconsin's system, and had some of the system's highest per-student costs. Through a maladroit effort to secure more funding, the school alienated powerful members of the legislature. As a result, it was forced to reduce its budget by a quarter, leading to widespread layoffs and cuts in programs. Having absorbed those cutbacks, however, Superior was positioned for a turnaround. With new leadership and a compelling initiative for academic renewal

(The Superior Plan), it experienced increased enrollment; more private support; an enhanced reputation; and consistent increases in state support. Several factors contributed to the turnaround, to be sure. But Superior's financial problems—and its response to them—were a felix culpa that paved the way for better times.

A similar pattern unfolded at the tiny University of Maine at Fort Kent. A bilingual campus in northern Maine, far closer to Montreal than to the state capital, Augusta, it has capitalized on its links to French-speaking Canada and its pristine location on the lovely St. John River to more than double enrollment and private giving and to increase state support as well. Charles Lyons, an energetic and imaginative leader, galvanized community support and enlisted the aid of an influential local legislator, John Martin, the former speaker of the Maine House of Representatives. Yet the resurgence would have been much more difficult had the campus not first reestablished its credibility by trimming nonessential programs and costs.

On a much larger scale, the mid-1990s turnaround in the fortunes of the public universities in Illinois happened only after a tough-minded state board insisted on massive cuts and resource reallocation. Under its "Priorities, Quality and Productivity" initiative, "some 300 university-level programs and 335 community college programs were eliminated, scaled back or consolidated," freeing up almost $400 million for new programs. That painful but necessary exercise in cost cutting restored the faith of legislators in public college and university management.[1] The cuts paved the way for increased state investments in higher education, investments well beyond the national average at the time. In the public sector, as in the private, then, the first stage in transforming lower-performing institutions begins with the credibility that hard financial choices bring.

Stage II: Marketing and Branding

We combine marketing and branding together in defining the second major stage because they work in parallel ways. For a school with its back to the wall, marketing to bring in fresh revenue must be the first priority. Branding is a longer-term effort and may have to be postponed until resources are available. A school may enjoy a splendid reputation or brand, but unless enough customers are able and willing to purchase its educational services, the school's image will suffer. Green Mountain College, for example, was once known as a safe and pleasant girls' finishing school where boys from Williams College came calling. But when women were admitted to Williams in 1970, Green Mountain's brand began to lose its power to attract students.

Marketing is the process of relating what an institution has to offer to groups of students, parents, employers, and others who will help pay for the service—or influence the students to seek it. In other words, marketing results in sales. Thus effective marketing may require adding new or improved educational products and services; communicating their value in more effective ways; adjusting the prices charged for them; and employing more analytical ways of segmenting and reaching markets—as well as a host of other strategies.

Brand is the image or reputation that the school holds in the minds of audiences, including prospective students. John Stuart, the onetime chairman of the Quaker Oats Company, famously said, "If the business were split up, I would take the brands, trademarks, and goodwill, and you could have the bricks and mortar—and I would do better than you."[2] Indeed, some institutions such as Quinnipiac University, in Connecticut, and Bentley College, in Massachusetts, left tired urban campuses behind but carried their reputations with them to new locations. A positive brand can also attract students who will never see a campus other than on its Web page. Still, unless a university's programs fulfill a need in the market and enough customers are willing to pay the price, brand is a worthless intangible.

Women's colleges throughout the country faced the problem of holding an attractive brand in a diminishing market. Some, such as Webster University, in an affluent suburb of St. Louis, were willing to sacrifice an increasingly hollow brand for revenue. Webster very successfully marketed graduate programs to adults around the country, and eventually around the world. Webster's sister institution, Loretto Heights College, in suburban Denver, also founded by the same Sisters of Loretto, was unable to make a transition and was eventually bought by neighboring Regis University.

Fusing an attractive brand with effective marketing strategies makes for a powerful tool to propel an institution forward within Stage II. Syracuse University has achieved momentum by branding itself as the best student-oriented research university and marketing itself to able students seeking that unique educational experience. The University of Connecticut is far along in a complete physical makeover of the campus, converting a dreary and uninspiring set of buildings into a truly splendid environment. The new plant yielded a successful rebranding for the university, moving it well ahead of its land-grant peers in New England. Connecticut is beginning its Stage III transformation into an academic powerhouse that promises to be as impressive as the campus that houses it.

Johnson & Wales University has grown from a proprietary business college in Providence, Rhode Island, to one of the nation's premier providers of graduates to the culinary and hospitality industries, shedding its for-profit status. It is relentless in branding itself as "America's Career University" and has attracted new students as well as many industry partners who employ its graduates.

Stage III: Strengthening Academic Programs and Culture

Stage III is the least businesslike phase of a turnaround, but success in that stage is often critical to sustaining the long-term health, financial and otherwise, of an institution. Stage III is also the most difficult and time consuming—and probably the least-often accomplished. At some institutions Stage III means a fundamental change in identity, mission, and educational programs. Northeastern University, in its move from an institution with nearly open admissions to a highly selective, top-notch research university, illustrates that kind of dramatic change. Others focus on strengthening features already present in the character of the place. Syracuse University's attention to becoming the nation's preeminent student-centered research university displays an emphasis on virtues already inherent in an institution.

It is easy to mistake achievements in Stage II for the more profound transformations of Stage III. To oversimplify a bit, Stage II is about appearances; Stage III is about substantive change. Several characteristics set Stage III apart from the earlier phases. In it, the energy and attention of senior leaders focus on changing internal beliefs, values, and interactions rather than on changing outside opinions. The goal is a profound and long-lasting alteration or strengthening of the organization itself—not merely the appearance of change. The quality of educational effort; the relations between faculty and students; the attitudes of all members of the community toward their work; ideas about what makes effective education; and a receptivity to candid self-appraisal are all Stage III features.

To be sure, success in Stage III manifests itself in the externalities of Stage II. A college that deeply engages its students in the life of the campus, both within and without the classroom; that challenges them academically; and that suggests a sense of social purpose beyond earning and spending will also exercise powerful appeal in the market for able students. Marketing goes a lot further when there is substantive evidence of educational effectiveness to report. High graduation and retention rates; impressive scores on graduate admissions tests and licensure exams; and evidence of student satisfaction and engagement are all products of Stage III improvements. Those and similar indicators are worth touting to prospective students and parents as well and contribute mightily to perceptions of educational value.

The case of Elon University, in North Carolina, reveals how Stage II and Stage III are intertwined. In a lovely book on Elon's transformation, George Keller chronicles the change from what one observer described as "a small, unattractive, parochial bottom-feeder" to one of the most distinctive colleges on the eastern seaboard.[3]

Founded by the United Church of Christ in 1889, Elon's formal links with the church attenuated over time. Nonetheless, the college continues to embody much of the communal and service-oriented spirit mission of its founders. One of the college's presidents underscores the continuity with the past in describing the "Elon Experience": "We chose four values—work, service, leadership, and cultural understanding—and made them the modern college's equivalent of old-time religious inculcation." The communal spirit thrives at Elon, and U.S. News & World Report has listed it as one of the 25 most interesting schools in the country.

If Stage III transformations reveal a consistency with historic missions, they also disclose an obsessive attention to reorienting virtually all dimensions of an institution to underscore a revised identity. From deciding who to admit, who to compete with in athletics, what courses and majors to offer, what faculty to hire, to the color of brick on new buildings—and nearly every other discretionary action—the most successful Stage III schools are relentless in their commitment to focused improvement across the board.

Few schools illustrate that total commitment to excellence as fully as Quinnipiac University, in Hamden, Connecticut. The following goals are taken from Quinnipiac's "Strategic Plan for Achieving Excellence and National Prominence."

- Achieve top ranks for all professional schools and divisions relative to their competitors.
- Identify and support selected programs that have the potential to achieve national prominence.
- Recruit and retain faculty of exceptional quality in all areas. All future appointments must possess the highest degree in their fields, and such degrees must be from top-tier universities and programs.
- Identify areas in need of improvement in faculty relations, teaching/research, etc., necessary to attract, retain, and support a faculty of exceptional ability to create and maintain a culture of excellence for all faculty in all academic programs.

FIRST THINGS FIRST

The experience of turnarounds strongly suggests that when budget problems are severe, the more painful tasks—cutting costs, programs, and staff, for example—must precede the more creative ones like marketing new programs. It is almost pointless to engage in a major rebranding exercise while a college is still hemorrhaging cash. And trying to redefine the academic culture of a university without first determining if there is a market for the new approach amounts to a tragic waste of time.

Faced with a dramatic decline in enrollment from its traditional clientele of young, middle-class, white women, a small eastern college continues to burn through its endowment and reserves without establishing a business model that leads to a balanced budget. Instead, it has pursued low-income students who have little capacity to pay the school's expensive tuition. That noble endeavor enjoys the support of the campus community, as well as of the trustees, and is entirely consistent with its historic mission. Yet the failure to first address the budget deficits suggests that the college has a high probability of going out of business once its reserves are exhausted, which is likely to be only a few years from now.

There are numerous stories of light-headed presidents seeking a different brand for their institution rather than addressing the truly critical financial challenges. A president of a "college of commerce," for example, tried to convert it into a graduate research institution. Not surprisingly, the effort failed in every way. The faculty, terrified at the prospect of losing their jobs, eventually forced out that executive.

A former president at Green Mountain College sought to rebrand the liberal arts college as the school of choice for the young, affluent, and athletic set that frequented the Mount Killington ski area by building a satellite campus there. With a mere handful of students, and substantial monthly debt payments, that marketing and branding failure exacerbated Green Mountain's already precarious financial state. However, as chapter 3 suggests, the larger rebranding of the college as what one observer described as an "environmentally friendly, L. L. Bean clothing sort of place" meant that the turnaround president, who successfully addressed the Stage I problems, did not need to invent a new image as well.

For institutions with serious financial problems, success lies in doing first things first. In such instances, the creative work of marketing and branding, as well as efforts to strengthen the academic culture, become possible only after achieving the discipline that results in a balanced budget.

Stage I Institutions

Many small, unselective private institutions remain frozen in Stage I. In retail terms, such schools resemble neighborhood convenience stores: they vend an adequate curriculum at a price much below the elite privates, though somewhat higher than the publics with the same degrees. In place of distinction, they offer useful educational services in applied fields of business, health care, graphic arts, or environmental studies—even occasionally in specialties such as aviation or law enforcement. Some of these Stage I schools are highly distressed. Others make a good living as their business-savvy leaders, perhaps abetted by a modest endowment or an able grant writer, deliver consistently balanced budgets.

But those most endangered of that species are only a dozen or so students away from extinction. A trustee at one of those schools characterized it as having a "culture of crisis," where looming deficits, or slower than expected deposits, or some other unexpected event led to a scurry of activity that, at the eleventh hour, bought reprieve. Upsala College of New Jersey; Bradford College, near Boston; Trinity College, in Burlington, Vermont; and Spring Garden College, in suburban Philadelphia typify the dangers of being mired in Stage I. According to Michael Townsley, all those schools succumbed because they carried "too much debt, too little cash, and too little skepticism by boards and presidents."[4]

Chronically on the watch lists of accreditation associations and federal financial aid authorities, the most fragile institutions endure long sentences under various levels of sanctions. But the U.S. Department of Education is pressuring accrediting bodies into making tougher decisions and granting shorter probationary terms. As a result, the next few years will likely witness the demise of more schools that lose accreditation.

For every failure of a Stage I institution, there are multiple examples of success stories. Some Stage I schools remain cheerfully unpretentious about moving up in the rankings, if they are even ranked at all. But they consistently turn in surplus budgets by providing their customers with what they want, at a price they are willing to pay.

Still another group of Stage I institutions flirt with the idea of branding but do not forget the primacy of the bottom line. Husson College, in Maine, is moving to Stage II from a now-solid financial base. During his first week as president in the late 1980s, Bill Beardsley learned that the college was in default on a HUD loan; the bank was withdrawing its line of credit; and the New England accrediting association was questioning Husson's credentials. From that inauspicious start, Beardsley has multiplied enrollment; bought a profitable school of communications; and begun to generate substantial cash surpluses, all while erecting an attractive new classroom building. By any measure, Husson is a successful Stage I institution.

But in 2005, the venerable but financially troubled Bangor Theological Seminary negotiated a move from near downtown Bangor to the Husson campus. Suddenly faculty were talking about Husson *University*. And the addition of doctoral programs as its first professional degrees in health sciences has fueled those discussions further. Identifying the right brand qualities for a regional school that also prides itself on being an "opportunity college" for local students is no easy task, but clearly Husson is enjoying—and being perplexed by—its Stage II options.

TRANSITIONS TO STAGES II AND III

Few universities have illustrated both the immense rewards that flow from successful turnarounds and the price fame demands as did New York University in its meteoric rise. NYU also illustrates one of the ambiguities surrounding Stages II and III: can we always distinguish between *looking* better and actually *being* better?

In a brilliant elegy for higher education that has given itself over to the market, David Kirp and his collaborators chronicle the transformation of NYU from a commuter school to "the success story in contemporary American higher education."[5] NYU suffered profound financial trauma from 1964 through the 1970s. Budget deficits of nearly $32 million led to widespread faculty and staff layoffs and to speculation that "the university might be going bankrupt."[6] Unexpected luck, and a remarkable leader, former U.S. congressman John Brademas, intervened to right the financial situation and eventually rebrand NYU as the home of academic all-stars.

The Mueller Macaroni Company, bequeathed to the university's law school, was sold for $115 million, with $40 million of that going to the university, in exchange for near full autonomy for the law school. Those monies solved the short-term financial problem, but Brademas's success as a fund-raiser provided the springboard for NYU's leap into a new level of preeminence. By the mid-1990s, Brademas had raised more than $1 billion from private sources and established a new high water mark for giving to NYU. Instead of banking the money in endowment, NYU "spent most of it on building and buying new facilities, and recruiting new faculty."[7]

NYU's rebranding and academic-enhancement strategy was to hire the best faculty it could find for selected departments and then give them modest teaching assignments, mostly in graduate seminars. That strategy catapulted NYU quickly to the top tier. The philosophy department, for example, moved within the span of five years from being a decimated unit lacking prestige and recognition to, by some accounts, the best in the country.

In Kirp's estimation, however, NYU has paid a substantial price for its success in the marketplace. "One consequence," he writes of the university's heavy-handed tactics, "is the absence of any sense of the commons."[8] If NYU is renowned for a star faculty with the resources and time to present and publish, it is also known as the first independent university to be forced by the courts to negotiate with its graduate assistants after they unionized.[9] NYU also employs the largest adjunct faculty unit of the United Auto Workers. The "teaching underclass" of adjuncts and graduate assistants is intertwined with the star faculty in Kirp's view.[10]

Success at Stage II branding has propelled NYU up the academic food chain, but according to Kirp, and to many of the insiders he interviewed, it exacerbated the fragmentation that is always a threat to academic community at metropolitan universities. Kirp quotes an unhappy faculty member who insists that the administration has sacrificed "substance in order to purchase cachet."[11] In our terms, that professor sees attempts at Stage III transformation as mere window dressing, aimed at presenting NYU as better than it really is. Other observers, however, argue that NYU has always had a contentious environment, and that amid the discord, the university has become a substantially better educational institution. The current president, John Sexton, a former dean of the university's law school, is working strenuously to restore a sense of community and to build a consensus that the new NYU is the right NYU.

SUCCESS BEGETS SUCCESS: THE POWER OF THE TURNAROUND CIRCLE

Achievement of each stage prepares the way for engaging in the next. The operating surpluses or risk capital generated in Stage I create the cash needed to design and market new programs and to begin developing a more positive brand (Stage II). Success in reaching new audiences not only generates resources but also is important in forcing an expansion of the idea of the institution and its mission (Stage III). Formal mission changes follow the creation of new programs. The combination of resources to invest; a growing feel for the potential in various markets, along with the confidence that success engenders; a larger vision of what a college is capable of being and doing; and the ability to attract more qualified and imaginative leaders all combine to help aspiring institutions become stronger and better.

The Turnaround Circle (Figure 1.1) suggests several realities of the turnaround. First, while the stages usually must be accomplished sequentially, leaders need to pay attention to each of the preceding ones as an institution progresses. Attractive brand recognition doesn't mean that the bottom line will take care of itself. And a preconception of the mission and culture requires that a revised identity be communicated effectively and realized in academic offerings (Stage II). Finally, a redefined

Figure 1.1 The Turnaround Circle

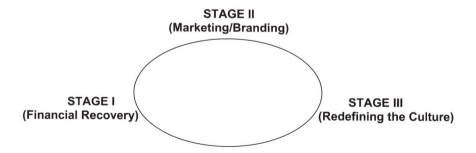

STAGE II
(Marketing/Branding)

STAGE I
(Financial Recovery)

STAGE III
(Redefining the Culture)

teaching learning model (Stage III) must make sense as a business model (Stage I) if the institution is to remain solvent.

The second reality is the mutually reinforcing energy of high performance at the three stages. Stage I generates cash to invest in marketable new or revised programs, just as a reputation for financial soundness contributes to a powerful brand for the institution. That in turn generates more revenue; provides more freedom to discount less; strengthens confidence of debt holders; and makes a school more attractive to donors and friends. The turnaround story becomes part of the university saga. The college is seen as on the move, having momentum, and doing exciting things. That public image becomes internalized and strengthened in Stage III, as an institution redefines its understanding of itself, changes its mode of behaving, and raises its aspirations for its future.

There is a magical quality to high-performing Stage III colleges and universities: everything seems to go right. Quinnipiac University, under the leadership of John Lahey, displays the powerful synergy among the stages. When Lahey joined Quinnipiac in 1987, he followed a president whose vision was to convert the former business college into a graduate research institution. Lahey brought a more realistic, yet ambitious, agenda to the campus. The college, which is now a university, enjoyed stable finances, so the Stage I process of realigning the budget with new priorities was not especially painful. Lahey focused initially on making the campus more attractive. Soon the temporary buildings disappeared. Today Quinnipiac looks like a classic New England liberal arts college, albeit without much ivy.

While Quinnipiac offers an attractive venue for parents and students who like the liberal arts model of a college, it also offers several career-oriented curricula, coupled with high standards. The guidelines for assuring excellence listed earlier demonstrate Lahey's systematic approach to improving Quinnipiac's standing. On the academic side, the addition of a law school, which was formerly part of the University of Bridgeport, and its rapid approval by the American Bar Association have added to Quinnipiac's cachet. Similarly, Lahey has added 18 graduate programs. The university's prestige has also been enhanced through athletics. Where its opponents were once regional state schools, Quinnipiac now fields a lacrosse team that attracts students from eastern prep schools and competes with Harvard on the field.

Quinnipiac is run like a business, but a business that intends to compete with the top tier of its peers. Lahey has built the quasi-endowment from operating surpluses, while using debt to enhance the facilities. While it does carry a fair amount of debt—much of it self-liquidating through residence fees—Quinnipiac's endowment balances out that liability. One result of that high debt/high endowment model is that the university enjoys a solid bond rating. As a successful Stage III institution, Quinnipiac can fill its freshman class with students paying (before financial aid) about $35,000 a year and can use its budget surplus to continue to enhance both quality and its reputation for quality.

Quinnipiac demonstrates the power of a successful Stage III institution where stronger academic quality reinforces the image of the school and enables it to charge substantial tuition. Thanks to tough-minded management, the school is able to channel those resources into an even stronger academic program and a more attractive, better-equipped campus. The results of the turnaround circle are born out in the metrics Quinnipiac uses to evaluate its progress.

The matrix depicted in Table 1.1 summarizes features of many turnarounds. Examining an institution's progress in terms of those seven variables—locus of attention, presidential leadership styles, trustee roles, faculty roles, academic changes, turning points between stages, and indicators of success—will help inform discussions of its position on the turnaround trajectory.

Responsibilities of Leaders

As this book emphasizes, Stage I must be about curing financial ills. It is the essential first step for schools with deficit budgets. Stage II focuses on the world outside the campus boundary by marketing programs and developing an attractive brand for the college. In Stage III the focus shifts inward to the academic life of the institution.

Leaders of the most thoughtfully planned turnarounds simultaneously think ahead to the next stage while immersed in the work of the primary one. Thus while Shaw at Syracuse was reducing and reallocating the budget (Stage I), he anticipated the rebranding of the research university as one oriented to students

Table 1.1 The Turnaround Matrix: Features of Each Stage

	Stage I Financial Recovery	Stage II Marketing and Branding	Stage III Redefining Academic Culture
Locus of Attention	Financial condition	Perceptions and choices of external audiences	Academic programs, culture, and community
Presidential Styles	Autocratic	Problem solving	Collaborative
Trustee Roles	Fiduciary	Relational	Strategic
Faculty Roles	Accept and legitimize broad policy changes	Develop and offer new programs	Strengthen the teaching-learning process
Academic Change	Downsizing and eliminating programs	Developing and marketing programs	Implementing new concepts of teaching and learning
Turning Points	Within two years	Within two years	Second year and beyond
Indicators of Success	Improvements in the CFI and other financial indicators	Enrollment and market measures	Higher scores on surveys of student engagement, satisfaction, and achievement

(Stage II and Stage III) by investing some of the freed-up funds in student affairs and in other quality initiatives. While the boundaries among the stages are porous, each stage must be substantially accomplished to provide a foundation for the succeeding one. That only occurs when leaders exhibit the discipline to both focus on the here and now *and* act with the future in mind.

Presidential Styles

Tom Longin, one of the early contributors to the ideas in this book and a well-known consultant to turnaround colleges, offers an insightful take on how presidential leadership styles need to change as a school develops through the stages. Longin posits three "dominant traits" in turnaround leaders: the autocratic chief executive; the pragmatic manager or problem solver; and the planning-oriented, collaborative leader.[12]

The Autocrat—A Stage I Persona
In Longin's scheme, the autocrat is a command-and-control type, one who abhors the very idea of shared governance. He or she is often demanding, manipulative, domineering, and insists on being the center of all decisions. That kind of executive uses the trustees more as a support group and cheering section than as friendly critics and advisers. Faculty members are nowhere near the inner decision-making circle. In such an environment, some faculty may profess respect for the executive, but that admiration is often mixed with a strong dose of fear as well.

But dire circumstances sometimes call for dire remedies. Indeed, a dictatorial leadership style sometimes works in the short run, particularly when draconian cuts are needed. According to Longin, however, that approach will not carry an institution forward to the stages that enhance a school's reputation or reinvigorate its educational programs. Some trustees subscribe to the myth that a "take charge, and take no prisoners" president is just the person to turn a failing institution around. The cases of successful turnarounds in this book, however, suggest that a dictatorial style is seldom the right one to improve the reputation and the performance of a school over the long term.

The Pragmatic Manager—A Stage II Type
The dominant responsibilities of a Stage II leader, as Longin sees them, are to focus on current problems, to seek quick fixes rather than longer-lasting solutions, and to see each task as discrete rather than connected to other facets of institutional life. If an autocrat likes to call attention to himself, a manager is self-effacing, comfortable with small work groups, and willing to share credit for successes. Such a type usually works effectively with trustees on well-defined problems such as financial aid and fund-raising. The faculty often appreciates his or her contributions to stability, at least for a time. The good manager elicits some gratitude, but seldom reverence.

The demands of Stage II often require the competence and patience of a pragmatic manager. Repositioning a college in the marketplace certainly calls for creativity, but given market-research techniques, it also demands quantitative and methodical planning. A journeyman manager for the work of Stage II seldom has the vision to carry an institution through the profound academic changes of Stage III.

The Collaborative Leader—A Person for All Stages

Longin's collaborative leader is a Renaissance individual, one with a broad range of intellectual, social, and emotional versatility. He or she is an accomplished communicator, invites participation across the board, and builds consensus around a shared sense of the institution's mission and values. Finally, a collaborative leader is unafraid of assessment of performance, and even of criticism, believing that such feedback leads to better performance.

That kind of leader subscribes to Jim Collins's view that selecting and supporting who does the work should come before deciding what exactly the work will be.[13] Thus a collaborative leader builds a strong, high-performing board and expects trustees to engage in vigorous discussion and debate. He or she views the faculty as partners, and in so doing helps them to strengthen educational and research programs.

Lest any of those portraits seem too stereotyped, Longin hastens to add some caveats. "Few presidents," he says,

> can be "confined" to or "defined" by a specific profile at a moment in time or over a long tenure. Indeed, presidents often manifest traits from one or both of the non-dominant profiles, or gradually move from one dominant profile to another over the course of a longer term in office—due either to a "hardening" or "softening" of dominant traits with age and/or experience or due to substantial changes in the environment.

He characterizes those presidential features as a "convenient means of communicating" about presidential leadership behaviors as an institution migrates through the changes required for a turnaround. And while the "collaborative leader" may seem too good to be true, the vast majority of successful turnaround leaders depicted in this book conform to that model—at least on their many good days.

Trustee Roles

The trustee responsibilities discussed in this book owe much to the groundbreaking ideas of Richard Chait, William Ryan, and Barbara Taylor.[14] Chait and his associates categorize trustee responsibilities as fiduciary (overseeing the management and allocation of resources); strategic (setting directions for the future of the enterprise based on an analysis of its strengths and weaknesses and its operating environment); and generative (which might be summarized as high-level brainstorming).

In this book, we redefine those roles somewhat and link them to discrete stages in the turnaround process. Not surprisingly, as the budget is being put to rights in Stage I, trustees need to be deeply engaged in their fiduciary role. A second set of responsibilities requires the board to use its prestige and connections to strengthen important relationships: linkages to donors, to political leaders and opinion makers, to government approval agencies, and, when necessary, to accrediting associations. Restoring or modifying an institution's reputation or brand, which we define as a Stage II activity, rests on a relationship between the college and its several markets. Trustees need to understand the value of their institutional brand, as well as their duty to sustain and strengthen it.

That responsibility includes a conventional understanding of strategic thinking based on an assessment of institutional strengths and weaknesses, and matched to analyses of environmental opportunities and threats, but also goes beyond it. As Richard Morrill points out in his thoughtful work on trusteeship, to fulfill their strategic responsibilities, trustees "must understand, monitor, evaluate, and exercise responsibility for the institution's academic programs and policies."[15] Traditionally, trustees have left the workings of educational programs to the academics. To be sure, faculty members are the right ones to determine who meets the standards for tenure and to set curricula. But because a turnaround can be incomplete without the academic revitalization of Stage III, trustees must be conversant with the strategic academic issues such as which programs to offer, build up, or reduce; the overall quality of programs in comparison with peers; and the linkages between academic programs, finances, and reputation in the marketplace.

Faculty Roles

Faculty members are highly engaged in successful turnarounds, although their roles change with each stage. During Stage I changes, faculty often endorse the tough decisions, though they are not typically consulted about which individuals should leave. To be sure, such participation is more the case at independent schools, which do not have unions or consistent streams of cash, than at public institutions with collective bargaining and a safety net of state funding. Where faculty collectively appreciate the precariousness of their situation, and come to believe that hard choices now will mean a brighter future, they tend to legitimize the process. That is clearly the case in the three Stage I turnaround cases presented in the next chapter.

As a turnaround migrates to Stage II, faculty ideas for marketing new or revised programs, as well as implementing them, are central. And in Stage III, faculty are not so much brought along but rather become the leaders in educational reform and revitalization. The College of New Jersey, while blessed with a string of capable administrative leaders, illustrates the multiple important roles of the professorate in moving an institution from mediocrity to excellence.

Academic Program Change

To bring about a stronger enterprise with a brighter future, educational programs must be altered. Stage I often encompasses program elimination and downsizing. It is also when the best programs with solid potential for attracting more students are protected, or improved, with freed-up resources. With its focus on improving a school's external reputation, Stage II is the time when a university creates—or enhances—programs with strong market appeal.

The academic changes of Stage III may have less to do with new curricula than with rethinking how teaching and learning occur within an established set of programs. Here the questions focus on how understandings of teaching and learning can be deepened; and they often include what should be taught as well. As opposed to asking what market will respond to a new MBA program, the academic question appropriate to Stage III might be "What values will a competent business leader need in the twenty-first century?"

Turning Points

There is no inevitable schedule for moving among the stages. The good fortune of an unanticipated gift, or some piece of bad luck such as the premature departure of a leader, may accelerate or delay progress. Some institutions linger in the first or second stage for years before a new leader emerges to spark upward movement again.

But after recognizing that the unexpected probably occurs more often than not, it still seems reasonable for trustees and regulators to look hard for evidence of progress within the time frames noted here. Decisive action on Stage I financial problems must occur within the first year, and the positive *results* from those actions should be apparent in the second year of the turnaround. Changes in marketing and branding strategy should begin in the later phases of the financial turnaround and should show results soon afterward. While the full flowering of Stage III changes in institutional personality bloom on forever, the practical steps of meeting, discussing, and changing the academic metabolism should begin no later than year two.

Indicators of Success

Well-resourced institutions can afford sophisticated institutional and market-research data to help fix their current positions as well as to progress. Until fairly recently, however, less well-heeled schools have been forced to rely on their own, often inadequate, data or even hearsay evidence about competing institutions.

Fortunately, there are now reliable and relatively inexpensive metrics to measure progress at each stage. The Composite Financial Index, along with the other measures Michael Townsley presents in chapter 5, encompasses the appropriate measures for Stage I. Those will continue to be necessary to assess the institution's continuing financial health through all the stages. Enrollment and retention figures, as well as market approval ratings based on surveys, become the quantitative indicators of success in Stage II. Measures of student engagement and satisfaction that allow benchmarking with peer and competing schools are now tested and available. The Association of Governing Boards offers to its members inexpensive and user-friendly benchmarking services, based on data collected by the federal government. The U.S. Department of Education makes available data that allow institutions to compare themselves with peers, and aspirational peers, on a variety of benchmarks. There is no longer any excuse for presidents and trustees—even those at the most impoverished schools—not to have access to, and use, quantitative measures of performance.

SUMMARY

The three stages of turnarounds appear in some degree at most colleges and universities experiencing a transformation. Restoring fiscal stability, marketing and branding an institution, and planning strategies for its future represent not only key turnaround emphases but also the work of competent and thoughtful leaders.

NOTES

1. Terrence J. MacTaggart and James R. Mingle, *Pursuing the Public's Agenda: Trustees in Partnership with State Leaders* (Washington, DC: The Association of Governing Boards of Colleges and Universities, 2002), 20.

2. James Twitchell, *Branded Nation: The Marketing of Megachurch, College, Inc., and Museumworld* (New York: Simon & Schuster, 2004), 20.

3. Ibid., 21.

4. Michael T. Townsley, *The Small College Guide to Financial Health: Beating the Odds* (Washington, DC: National Association of College and University Business Officers, 2002), 89.

5. David Kirp, Elizabeth Popp Berman, Jeffrey T. Holman, Patrick Roberts, Debra Solomon, and Jonathan VanAntwerpen, *Shakespeare, Einstein, and the Bottom Line: The Marketing of Higher Education* (Cambridge, MA: Harvard University Press, 2004), 66.

6. Ibid., 70.

7. Ibid., 66.

8. Ibid., 87.

9. Ibid.

10. Ibid., 69.

11. Ibid., 74.

12. Thomas C. Longin, "Styles of Turnaround Leadership" (Regis College, unpublished presentation, June 14, 2004).

13. Jim Collins, *Good to Great and the Social Sectors* (self-published monograph, 2005), 41.

14. Richard Chait, William Ryan, and Barbara Taylor, *Governance as Leadership: Reframing the Work of Nonprofit Boards* (Hoboken, NJ: John Wiley & Sons, 2004).

15. Richard Morrill, *Strategic Leadership in Academic Affairs: Clarifying the Board's Responsibilities* (Washington, DC: The Association of Governing Boards of Colleges and Universities, 2002), xv.

CHAPTER 2

Critical Success Factors in Restoring Financial Health

Terrence MacTaggart

"Chainsaw Al" Dunlap fired 11,000 employees immediately upon taking over Scott Paper in 1994. He quickly sold off several of Scott's businesses. "Shareholders are the number one constituency," Dunlap asserted. "Show me an annual report with six or seven constituencies, and I'll show you a mismanaged company."[1] In less than two years, the value of Scott Paper tripled to about $9 billion. Dunlap's slash-and-burn tactics created wealth for stockholders but did not create an enduring organization. Dunlap "failed to build the capabilities needed for sustained competitive advantage—commitment, coordination, communication and creativity."[2] In 1995, Kimberly-Clark acquired its longtime rival in the paper business.

Dunlap's extreme tactics underscore key differences between corporate and academic turnarounds. While Stage I changes are about finances, their purpose is to restore health to the institution—not to prepare it for a sale. Colleges and universities have at least six or seven constituencies, but they can't be mismanaged and survive. If Stage I turnarounds were only about converting the income statement from red to black, they would be difficult enough. But in making the hard choices that Stage I restorations require, the best leaders realize that those choices represent only a *stage* in the growth process. Even as people are laid off and programs are discontinued, the most adroit Stage I leaders work to position the institution for a more robust future.

To be sure, many corporate transformations are about saving the business, not stripping its assets for quick sale. And some academic turnarounds require a significant dismemberment. Trustees of Goddard College faced the prospects of going bankrupt or of selling off the campus and its programs. Beset with a low student-faculty ratio and a relatively expensive full-time faculty, the traditional undergraduate program could not be sustained. There were questions regarding continued accreditation. Ultimately, the college shut down its undergraduate program in favor of a low-residency alternative for older students. Closing the traditional program and dismissing its faculty saved the college, and today it is a going concern.

CRITICAL SUCCESS FACTORS

There is a pattern in successful Stage I turnarounds: five elements seem always to be present. Trustees hire new leaders unfettered by past decisions or relationships. Those presidents and chancellors demand accurate, timely financial information and analysis. The institution addresses the immediate financial challenges decisively, but in a way that sustains core values. Transparency characterizes both the presentation of the financial problems and the hard choices. Finally, faculty are engaged in many of the decisions that ultimately right the institution.

To illustrate the complexities of cutting programs and faculty in order to grow, we focus on the Stage I experiences of very different institutions: Green Mountain College, in Poultney, Vermont; Syracuse University, in Syracuse, New York; and Regis College, in the Boston suburb of Weston. As distinctive as those independent schools are, they each illustrate the five universal success characteristics of Stage I change in the independent sector.

New Leaders

No president who participated in the decline was able to subsequently lead the turnarounds described in this book. The challenges demanded a new leader. Green Mountain, Syracuse, and Regis each attracted a new president who displayed just the right talent for the turnaround task at hand. As different as those three strong-willed people are, they share uncommon gifts for straight talk; hard-headed analysis of the problems, along with practical ideas on how to solve them; and a willingness to take decisive action.

We can only speculate as to why no incumbent president could lead a turnaround. In some instances, the president was viewed as the problem. The faculty, and eventually the trustees as well, lost confidence in the executive's ability to make the right moves. And besieged presidents often vest too much in a single new marketing ploy that fails altogether, or doesn't attract students quickly enough to stem the cash hemorrhage. Whatever the reasons, we found no instances of incumbent presidents being able to take the dramatic actions required in Stage I turnarounds. Of their own volition, or by board action, they had to go.

A partial, and interesting, exception to that rule is Jack Curry, who led the first phase of the turnaround at Northeastern University. As a vice president, Curry held office while both enrollments and finances plummeted. As president, he initiated dramatic changes that transformed Northeastern. Trustees seeking a turnaround leader are best advised not to look to the current chief executive, but as Curry illustrates, a talented senior administrator may be equipped to do the job.

Not surprisingly, chief financial officers played a critical role on new leadership teams. They also assumed broader responsibility. To be sure, solid and reliable financial information remained a core expectation. But the CFOs needed to be creative in identifying business opportunities such as developing college-owned real estate, refinancing debt, and negotiating with vendors to provide better service at lower cost. In fact, Tom Pistorino, the financial vice president at Regis College, believes that successful turnaround CFOs are not only book-keepers or CPAs but also business strategists.

In the early phases of the successful turnarounds we examined, the academic dean or vice president typically served as an important link to the faculty and to the larger academic community. Sometimes coming from the faculty itself, that person participated in the key decisions but also contributed a sense of legitimacy to the new regime.

Accurate and Timely Financial Information

Many fragile institutions simply do not know how much they are taking in or how much they are spending. Chronic deficits; the need to borrow regularly to meet payroll; the risk of default on debt; an increasing tuition discount rate to attract students; and downward enrollment and retention trends should set off strident alarms. An institution that cannot produce those numbers consistently and reliably is surely in worse shape than one that can, especially if the trends are negative.

Michael Townsley, in chapter 5, outlines several financial indicators and sources for many more that will enable executives and trustees to calibrate institutional financial health. He also describes, as he does in his widely read book *The Small College Guide to Financial Health*, a financial monitoring system that can be adapted to the information needs of almost any institution.[3]

Trustees, lenders, donors, and accreditors need to know the answers to key financial questions. Is an institution gaining or losing net wealth as the years go by? Is it living within its means? Can it meet it current and future obligations? Do the trends show that it is getting stronger or weaker financially? Trustees, and others needing a short list of indicators, can look to these numbers for a barometer of financial health:

- Trends in net assets
- Income from operations after expenses
- Unrestricted cash available from operations
- Ability to cover short term debt
- Actual tuition received per student after institutional aid
- Enrollment and retention trends

Actions Focused on Finances

Effective turnaround leaders resist being beguiled by initiatives whose payoff will come only in the sweet by and by. They do not confuse the demands of Stage I with opportunities to be pursued in Stage II. For example, a cash shortage that jeopardizes debt payments and threatens the school with foreclosure won't wait for a new marketing effort to yield more revenue. Jack Brennan knew that restoring positive cash flow had to precede new curricula at Green Mountain. He set the finances right before mounting new graduate degrees.

Of course, schools with available reserves can be less draconian in their cuts. Buzz Shaw told his staff at Syracuse that it was not essential that the budget be balanced in his first year, so long as there were firm plans to make the necessary reductions by year three. In fact, the budget was brought in line during the first 12 months. Mary Jane England, president at Regis, had the luxury of time, thanks to an unrestricted endowment, and ownership of some of the most expensive real estate in the Boston area. Even so, she laid off a third of the staff within six months of taking office.

Transparency

The pact between the leaders and the led at the schools includes a treaty of no surprises. Each new leader fully disclosed the seriousness of the problems to the trustees and the campus community. The dire facts came as no great surprise to the faculty at Green Mountain, who had been more alert to the problems than the board appears to have been. Mary Jane England enjoys strong support in her actions to restore a balanced budget, in part because all her moves are transparent. The vague awareness of fiscal distress that faculty and staff felt at Syracuse before Shaw arrived became very concrete as he made his way to each department with the facts and figures.

Faculty Involvement

Finally, and somewhat to our surprise, faculty and staff members at the three institutions played a substantive role in many of the difficult choices. The view that only a slash-and-burn manager can make the tough decisions required of Stage I is a myth. Successful turnaround leaders are more apt to share their purposes widely. They enlist not only their administrative team, but also the larger community in the process.

The politics of engagement requires finesse. At Green Mountain, faculty participated on the budget committee that made some of the cuts, but they did not have to vote on who lost a job or who kept one. Shaw specifically asked the senate at Syracuse not to vote on reductions that would imperil their colleagues. He explained that it would be unfair to ask the senate to advocate harm to their peers. In the event, his reductions totaling some $66 million were widely accepted as necessary by the campus community, including the faculty senate.

GREEN MOUNTAIN COLLEGE: A CLASSIC STAGE I TURNAROUND

In the unlikely event that Steven Spielberg produces a movie about college turnarounds, he would do well to cast Jack Brennan in the role of turnaround president. And he can shoot the film quickly, because his crew will have few distractions in the small, picturesque town of Poultney, Vermont.

"One Very Tough Irishman"

Described as "one very tough Irishman" who is also "very savvy and well connected in the Boston business community," Jack Brennan came to Green Mountain in the summer of 2002 with an attitude and experiences ideally suited to the life-threatening problems facing the college. Within a year, Brennan and his team turned the income statement from red to black, reduced $1.7 million in aged debt to $300,000, and resolved a $6 million lawsuit down to $300,000, which they promptly paid. Beyond such dramatic turning points, they laid the groundwork for upswings in enrollment, retention, and private giving.

Brennan had enjoyed a successful business and academic career before taking on the challenges at Green Mountain. His career included a Harvard MBA, a bank start-up, several corporate turnarounds, an endowed professorship in business at Skidmore College, and ten years as dean of the Sawyer School of Management at Suffolk University, in downtown Boston. In fact, Brennan hadn't been to Green Mountain since he was an undergraduate at nearby Williams College.

Skeptical of the school's chances for survival, Brennan refused to allow the search committee to contact his references until he had reviewed the audited financial statements. With a reluctance that is difficult to understand, the board eventually released the documents, and Brennan provided the references.

A Capable Financial Officer

Like Jim Collins in *Good to Great,* Brennan seems to believe the "who" is as important as the "what."[4] Brennan makes much of the contributions of his team. He had the good fortune to inherit as his CFO Joe Manning, a former banker who specialized in securing financing for small firms. Manning's skills in finance and his credibility with rural Vermont businessmen proved essential to Green Mountain. Manning is one of those gifted college CFOs whose skills transcend accounting to include strategic management. He negotiated substantial reductions in debt to local vendors, persuaded the bank to restructure other short-term debt into a long-term $9.3 million bond, and played a key role in resolving the multimillion dollar lawsuit.

Focus on Finances

Perhaps as important as the actions they took are the possibilities they chose to forgo. Brennan and his team remained focused on the critical problems facing the school: the potentially debilitating lawsuit, short-term debt, and other obligations to local merchants. They did not immediately change the curriculum, or expand programming, or engage in online delivery or other initiatives, under a rubric of growing out of the problem. To be sure, they emphasized recruitment and retention to the existing programs, and to the campus itself. Admissions grew from 176 to 340 between 2003 and 2005. An attrition rate of 50 percent between first- and second-year students has been cut nearly in half. And the college recently gained approval from its accrediting association to offer an MBA and

an MS in environmental studies. But the success of the Stage I turnaround rested
on improving the core business before engaging in new ventures.

Brennan's "stick to the basics" philosophy plays out in his penchant for measuring progress with financial ratios. Borrowing from his own business and academic
experiences, he regularly tracks performance in terms of net asset growth, return
on net assets, net income ratio, debt ratio, working capital ratio, tuition discount
ratio, and the CFI. (The CFI is the Composite Financial Index, which is discussed
extensively in chapter 5.)

A Knowledgeable and Engaged Faculty

It is difficult for outsiders to appreciate the capacity of some boards to refuse to
acknowledge the vulnerability of the institutions they are charged with overseeing. In a post–Sarbanes-Oxley world, even trustees of nonprofits are expected to
be more alert to their fiduciary obligations than some university boards of trustees.
The board at Green Mountain seems to have been denying the school's mounting
fiscal problems. But the faculty members were not. They went over the head of the
sitting president to tell the board of their concerns, and set in motion the chain
of events that brought Brennan to the presidency.

Candor about the financial realities is now characteristic at Green Mountain. In
place of the glowing bromides and lofty visions of most inaugural speeches, the new
president emphasized the fiscal mess, and his plans to address it. Brennan found
a receptive audience in the faculty, who fully realized that without tough management their vision of the environmental liberal arts college could not be sustained.

A senior professor described the remarkable academic culture at the college by
saying that faculty took ownership of the distress facing Green Mountain. They
appreciate that maintaining their niche as an environmental college located in a
small village in Vermont is not easy. Their commitment is typified in the belief,
as one faculty member put it, that "if things go bad, it's my fault, not just the
institution's."

After Brennan came on board, the academic community remained deeply
engaged in addressing the crisis. Faculty and staff belonged to the budget committee that did some of the painful work. Some staff members were laid off; contributions to the retirement system were suspended for eight months; and there were
draconian cuts in operating budgets. But no faculty members lost their jobs. Their
confidence in the institution and its leader remains unshaken. In maintaining
morale and in bringing about the necessary cuts, according to a senior professor,
"this transparency was critical."

"A Precious Thing"

To be sure, Green Mountain remains challenged. It is a small college at the far
end of a two-lane road. It enrolls about 700 students, despite ambitions to grow
to 1,000. Its endowment stands at a modest $2.3 million. The campus is too large
for the current enrollment. And although its nearly 10 million dollars worth of
debt has been rescheduled, the obligation remains.

Still, its future is brighter now than at any time in recent history. All of Jack Brennan's financial indicators show positive trends. There is a confidence about the place. Clearly, the Stage I work of establishing a realistic business plan for the college is complete, and, with the approval of the two new master's programs, it is moving on to Stage II.

Brennan recognized that ordering Green Mountain's finances represented a necessary step, but only a first step in the gradual revitalization of the college. When asked why Green Mountain was worth preserving, he observed, "This venerable institution is 170 years old. It is a noble thing. Every institution of learning is a precious thing."

SYRACUSE UNIVERSITY: A LEADING STUDENT-CENTERED RESEARCH UNIVERSITY

Buzz Shaw might not have appeared to be a logical choice for the chancellorship at Syracuse when he was selected in early 1991. Shaw had been a president at the University of Wisconsin, but he served as head of the Wisconsin *System*, not the research powerhouse in Madison. And his entire career had been spent at public institutions. A vice president and dean at Towson University, in Maryland, president of the Southern Illinois University campus in Edwardsville, and eventually head of the two-campus system that included Carbondale, Shaw seemed more suited for the political world of a Big 10 institution, or a large public system, than a distinctive private research university.

But the trustees who interviewed Shaw realized that he possessed the leadership traits needed to restore Syracuse. According to one observer, Shaw had "the fortitude to make hard choices and the charisma to persuade others to go along with him." In Wisconsin, he had instituted a tough program of enrollment cuts to match the reduced resources coming from the legislature. As unpopular as that initiative was, Shaw and his team felt it was essential to avoid dumbing down the university through a formula of too many students and too few full-time faculty members.

Shaw pursued a policy of rightsizing enrollment at Syracuse but added components designed to both enhance the university's reputation and strengthen its sense of community. In other words, he moved quickly to address Stage I financial problems but did so with an eye toward Stage II and III requirements. He made Syracuse a more attractive destination for higher quality students and refashioned its ethos to make it one of the nation's leading student-centered research universities.

"The Best State School I've Visited"

Outwardly, the university Shaw took over in August of 1991 seemed secure. The campus on a gentle hillside in urban Syracuse teemed with students, the men's and women's basketball teams were victorious (although there were NCAA violations to be managed), and healthy reserves compensated for a modest budget imbalance. The trends told a different story. From a report commissioned by his predecessor, Shaw learned that Syracuse was dipping deeper into its enrollment pool to fill the freshman class. Its reputation for quality attracted a large group of applicants, but many of the best students accepted other offers. And the reputation itself had begun to blur. In a telling remark, one prospective student praised the private university by saying, "This is the best state school I've visited."

To prevent those issues from morphing to a crisis, Shaw took his message personally to every college and school on the campus. He told the deans, the faculty, the students, and anyone else who would listen, that indeed the campus had a budget imbalance that needed correction, and that a school that was 85 percent dependent on income from students could not risk losing its market appeal. The challenges, he said, did not yet amount to a catastrophe, but they were serious. And he informed the campus community that each of its members would be engaged in putting the university on the right course.[5]

Smaller but Better

When Shaw arrived at Syracuse, the university registered about 13,500 students. In 2000, 11,500 students enrolled. There were fewer students, but they were better prepared for challenging academic work and more apt to remain through graduation. The budget shrank as well. By 1997, some $66 million had been cut from operating expenses. Although no tenured faculty members were dismissed, the faculty complement declined by 165, and about 400 staff departed as well. It is an understatement to say that those are significant numbers.

Several things are remarkable about the Stage I cuts at Syracuse. The reductions were selective and strategic. One unit lost nearly a third of its budget, but others gained some. The entire process was transparent. According to one member of Shaw's team, "We let it all hang out" by demonstrating both the institution-wide picture and the revenues and expenses of each college.

As Shaw had promised, he made the faculty part of the university's turnaround. But he did so without requiring anyone to vote on actions that would bring harm to his or her colleagues. The process was conducted with a strong sense of humanity that preserved—in some ways may have even enhanced—the bonds within the academic community. Layoffs of union members included provisions for priority in rehiring, for example. And supervisors who had to dismiss members of their staffs received special training in the process, with due attention to the dignity of employees, and, interestingly, to managing the complex emotions felt by the remaining staff.

Investments for the Future

Thanks to its healthy financial reserves, Syracuse could bear some short-term costs that would bring benefits down the road. Shaw invested $25 million in generous faculty buyouts. Academics who were paid less than the average and who met a length of service requirement could walk away with two years salary. While expensive, the process enabled some tenured faculty to leave without the agony of retrenchment. It also paved the way for some important new hires.

Shaw also invested in teaching. At the same time that some programs faced downsizing, the university invested $2 million over three years in improving undergraduate teaching. Shaw directed a timely, unrestricted gift of $5 million to develop Meredith Professors. The award provided a substantial add-on ($22,000) to the salaries, along with another $10,000 for professional expenses, of faculty recognized as excellent teachers.

In 1995, Syracuse publicly announced its goal of becoming the nation's best student-oriented research university, and invested in a variety of programs designed to more deeply engage students in their collegiate experience. Out of that initiative came 29 residential and nonresidential learning communities; a revised orientation program that required summer readings to be widely discussed in the fall; and the Center for Public and Community Service, which oversees more than a half million hours each year of student volunteer work, as well as courses with service-learning components.

Results That Count

Syracuse has become a smaller and better university. It now attracts more top students. It witnessed a 90 percent increase in students coming from the top decile of their high school class. The two-year attrition rate has improved by two-thirds; and the six-year graduation rate climbed from about 70 percent to better than 80 percent. Private giving is up substantially. And the school received the prestigious Hesburgh Award for creativity in developing faculty.

The Intentional Leader

In *The Intentional Leader*, Shaw aptly describes his own managerial style but also calls attention to several important features of the Syracuse story. By deliberately acting in time to prevent the slide toward mediocrity from becoming a collapse, Shaw and his team redeemed one of America's great private research universities. In addition to its timeliness, the turnaround at Syracuse developed in a manner at once humane, effective, and thoughtfully oriented toward building a stronger university. In the terms used in this book, the tough decisions that we describe as Stage I were conducted with the intention of positioning the university for Stages II and III. Reflecting on the transformation, Shaw observes, "We decided that this was an opportunity for renewal and transformation, understanding that cutting budgets alone would not serve to make us better."[6]

REGIS COLLEGE: EXCELLENCE WITH GENTLENESS

There is a moral fervor about Regis College, a small Roman Catholic women's college founded in 1926 by the Sisters of St. Joseph of Boston. Banners that line the drive leading to the campus's majestic central building witness that commitment. They read, "Welcoming All, Making a Difference, Loving God and Others, Excellence with Gentleness."

There is also a moral intensity about the college's new leader, Mary Jane England, a psychiatrist and an alumna of the class of 1959. A former commissioner for social services for Massachusetts, associate dean at Harvard's Kennedy School of Government, and president of a Washington-based association of business leaders dedicated to health care reform, England enjoyed substantial experience in both policy setting, and in managing large, complex public organizations. She had never run, much less turned around, a small college. What she did bring, along with her relevant background, was a commitment to empowering women, a concern for social justice, and a desire to find creative ways to deliver education and health care.

With that emotional investment, she also brought a dry-eyed appreciation for the task at hand. She wanted very much to stabilize the school's financial situation so that it could continue as a women's college.

But the long-term challenge facing England, Regis, and the dwindling number of Roman Catholic women's colleges, is to develop a business model that supports their original missions. For a time, Regis compromised by admitting men to its graduate and off-campus programs. Male students enrolled in the college's lifelong learning programs could also take courses in the undergraduate day program at the Weston campus. But Regis resisted becoming entirely coeducational, refusing to sacrifice one of its core values for the possibility of greater success in the marketplace.

Now, however, it plans to admit men to its undergraduate programs. Explaining the decision to *The Chronicle of Higher Education*, England noted, "We're tiny, and we need to be small ... to get more women, we know we need to admit men."[7] Regis is also banking on some familiar initiatives, such as appealing to working adult students and leveraging the college's unique assets, especially its sizable landholdings some 12 miles from the center of Boston, to restore fiscal stability.

Financial Exigency

When England returned to her alma mater she was greeted by an appreciative board and an optimistic faculty. She also faced declining enrollments, a deteriorating campus, debt with no obvious revenue source to redeem it, and a $6.8 million annual deficit. The operating loss alone represented about a fifth of the annual budget of less than $30 million.

In December 2002, she persuaded the board to declare financial exigency. A third of the faculty and staff were let go. Majors in chemistry, mathematics, economics, and French were eliminated, though many of their courses remained to service other majors. In a bold organizational restructuring, the academic program was consolidated from 26 departments into 6 centers.

The declaration of financial exigency gave the board and England great authority in making those changes. But they were handled with the "gentleness" that the campus prizes. Faculty, staff, and students participated in college-wide discussion groups that in some ways legitimated the hard decisions. While the 48 departures were not voluntary, the college did provide useful outplacement services and reasonable severance packages. Remarkably, there were no lawsuits instigated by the retrenchment.

By taking those Stage I actions quickly—they were completed within six months of her arrival—England could reassure the campus community in January 2002, telling its members that there would be no further layoffs.

A Five-Year Turnaround Plan

"Throwing furniture in the fireplace" is how Tom Pistorino, the college's CFO, describes the situation before he and England arrived within a month of each other. Now Regis moves purposefully in managing its finances. While the pace of change at Regis is not leisurely, still the college is pursuing a methodical five-year plan to what it hopes will be permanent stability. A largely unrestricted endowment that now totals about $20 million, cost cutting, some enrollment growth, and development of some of its real estate holdings all underpin the approach.

Some of the initiatives are predictable. Regis expanded programming to early- and mid-career men and women in health care and other fields. Accelerated degree completion programs are now available off campus. Thanks to those efforts, Regis now enrolls about a thousand adult learners. The traditional undergraduate program has reached 600 students, but its growth has been slower than expected. Signs of increased efficiency include a new faculty-student ratio of 1 to 13, up from 1 to 10. The teaching load has increased to four courses each term.

Leveraging Assets

In addition to an attractive campus, but one too large for its current study body, Regis holds title to some of the most expensive real estate in the greater Boston area. To leverage that asset, Regis has rented out residence hall space to another institution and made its spacious facilities available for conferences, weddings, and other social events. It sold one parcel of land for a single-family home—more likely, a mansion—for more than $9 million.

Regis's most ambitious idea for achieving financial stability while enhancing the education program is a senior citizen development called the East Campus Community. The concept is intriguing. On 68 acres near the Weston campus, Regis plans to develop an intergenerational community for residents averaging 70 years of age. Residents will enroll in courses at the college and participate in its cultural events. Students, especially those in the college's strong nursing and gerontology programs, will find work in their career fields near to their classrooms. In an aging, well-educated, and affluent Boston, such a facility could attract the kind of clientele it would need to succeed. It also represents a creative approach to delivering educational and health care services. The college's description of the project glows: "We further picture intimate interconnecting pathways making travel easier for those in wheelchairs, as well as for those with baby strollers, two-wheeled grocery carts, or canes, or walkers."[8]

Will It All Work?

There are limits to the cutting that is required in Stage I turnarounds. Regis has probably done nearly all it can to shrink costs.

The college community, and especially England and Pistorino, are fully aware that the financial turnaround remains incomplete. In the past dozen years, the endowment has declined from $36 million to $20 million. The deficits are shrinking but still running at $4 million annually. Enrollment has grown, private giving is up, and the college has received a $1.8 million Title III grant from the federal government. But that growth and the initiatives supported by the "strengthening developing institutions" grant have not yet led to a balanced budget.

Regis's calculation that the Stage I turnaround can be completed in five years rests on a combination of very tangible, and some less tangible, assets. At the time of this writing, the East Campus Community project remains a concept. The college is free to develop the community itself, to partner with a developer, or find other uses for the acreage. The asset, however, along with the remaining endowment, insulates Regis from bankruptcy any time soon.

Less tangible, but perhaps even more important, than the real estate is the realism that England and Pistorino bring to their analysis of Regis's progress. Pistorino in particular uses easily understood ratios and trends to inform the board and the college community precisely how much progress the college is making and where it needs to make more progress still. The college takes those numbers seriously.

Finally, the lofty purposes of the college, which England so often reiterates in her communications, constitute an important asset. The firm belief that small Regis College, located in the densely populated academic environment of Boston, still makes unique contributions to the lives of women, adult learners, and even to social policy for the elderly animates the work of the college and its dedicated supporters.

SUMMARY

The view of turnaround leaders as take-no-prisoners autocrats turns out to be a myth, at least when it comes to transforming colleges and universities. Effective leaders proceed thoughtfully with accurate financial information; focus on what will actually help in the short run, for example, the finances; are highly transparent in their work; and engage the faculty. They also know that what we have labeled Stage I, restoring financial health, is just the first act in a turnaround drama.

NOTES

1. Michael Beer and Nitin Nohria, "Cracking the Code of Change" (Cambridge MA: Harvard Business School, 2000). [Reprint # R00301] 7.

2. Ibid., 12.

3. Michael T. Townsley, *The Small College Guide to Financial Health: Beating the Odds* (Washington, DC: National Association of College and University Business Officers, 2002).

4. Jim Collins, *Good to Great and the Social Sectors* (self-published monograph, 2005).

5. Kenneth A. Shaw, *The Intentional Leader* (Syracuse, NY: Syracuse University Press, 2005), 149.

6. Ibid., 148.

7. Sara Lupka, "Regis College Decides to Admit Men in 2007," *The Chronicle of Higher Education*, September 15, 2006, 40.

8. Regis College, http://www.regiscollege.edu/eastcampus/index.html (retrieved January 2, 2007).

CHAPTER 3

Transforming Ugly Ducklings: Marketing and Branding the New American Colleges

Jerry Berberet

In a provocative and widely circulated 1990 essay, Frank Wong, provost at the University of Redlands, described the plight of the "ugly ducklings" of American higher education.[1] Such private colleges and universities were, in a phrase later applied by Ernest Boyer, hybrids. They offered too many undergraduate and graduate career-preparation programs to be regarded as pure liberal arts colleges. They emphasized the humanities too much to be primarily professional institutions. They paid too much attention to undergraduate students to be serious research universities. Their tuition was too high to compete aggressively with state institutions. The brood he described would have included Valparaiso University, in Indiana; Hamline University, in Minnesota; Ithaca College, in central New York; and Quinnipiac University, in Connecticut—among many others.

Although Wong labeled them as ugly ducklings, none were low-tier schools: they simply lacked a compelling story that would allow them to rise above their competition in the minds of prospective students.[2] They had not defined themselves by what they were—focused on community involvement, professional and liberal studies, and social progress—but had allowed themselves to be categorized as what they were not—too selective, too elitist, too expensive. They had great difficulty presenting the full range of virtues they possessed to traditional students, adult learners, or graduate students. In other words, they lacked a positive brand.

This chapter explains how some of those ugly ducklings have repositioned themselves as swans through able marketing and branding of their distinctive virtues. Although many of the institutions did not experience deep financial distress, their stories all illustrate the importance of marketing and branding.

The cases are relevant—indeed, inspiring—because they show that marketing and branding are about matching bona fide institutional strengths with market needs and preferences. The stories the schools present to prospective students, donors, and others enjoy, in Henry Kissinger's words, the advantage of being true. A brand is really a promise to consumers that they will actually experience what they have been led to believe about a service, product, or organization. And the stories in this chapter represent success at turning negatives into positives in the minds of students, donors, and a university's additional constituencies.

SOME DEFINITIONS

Since American higher education has become immersed in "the ethos of capitalist competition," the practices of marketing and branding long applied in business have migrated to colleges and universities.[3] As the number of books, articles, presentations, and consultants on those topics has multiplied, so have the difficulties in defining them. What follows are basic definitions of the terms as used in this chapter.

"Marketing" is all the activities a school engages in to persuade potential students to enroll. The most effective marketing begins with honest reflection on what assets a school possesses, or can readily develop, to meet needs and demands of students. That intellectual and reflective process is followed, and modified, by a nearly infinite number of strategies. Thus under the rubric of marketing we include market research, message development, advertising, view books, admissions processes, student preference and satisfaction surveys, service audits, branding strategies, curriculum creation and redesign, residence hall and recreational center renovations, retention strategies—just about anything that might encourage students to enroll and reenroll.

"Market" refers to the set of individuals that the college seeks to attract: its needs, wants, and sense of identity. Do its ideal students want a small campus with small classes? A highly personalized campus environment? Big-time football? Outdoor recreation and skiing? A rigorous academic program? Close contact with faculty? A brand-name degree? Do those ideal students have high test scores? A strong sense of social justice? An interest in particular academic curricula? Marketing enables an institution to reach the target market of students most likely to be attracted to, and benefit from, what it has to offer.

Most institutions find themselves in something of a buyer's market in which schools compete with one another to attract at least minimally qualified students. The large group that Twitchell characterizes as lower-echelon mass providers—including Marquette University, Georgia State University, and Colorado State University—is still seeking students to fill their entering classes well into the summer.[4]

The elite or brand-name schools are also in the market for students, but for the best students. The most prestigious schools need top students every bit as much as the top students need them; they must maintain their reputation as elite.[5] Thus every higher education enterprise, from the Ivy to the local state school, needs to reach its market.

"Branding" is a marketing strategy. It includes all institutional actions aimed at creating an idea, a set of impressions, a story that defines that institution in the minds and hearts of student-consumers. A name change is the most visible branding tactic. For example, the state teachers colleges in Pennsylvania all became universities (such as Slippery Rock State College, now Slippery Rock University of Pennsylvania). Substituting the College of New Jersey for Trenton State College and shifting from North Adams State College to Massachusetts College of Liberal Arts were dramatic examples of rebranding. In a famous example of changing a label to change perception, Beaver College, in Pennsylvania, became Arcadia University. Along with other stratagems, the new name led to a sharp increase in first-year enrollment.[6]

"Brand" is the collection of impressions and attitudes that exists in the minds of consumers. A brand emerges partly as a consequence of deliberate branding efforts but also from a variety of influencers beyond an institution's control. The reputation (a close synonym for brand) of those southern colleges damaged by Hurricane Katrina in 2005 will be diminished for some time as potential students harbor images of flooded campuses and ravaged buildings, for example. Of course, if they spring back quickly, as California State University at Northridge did following a destructive earthquake, the damage to their brands need not persist too long after the campuses are repaired.

Successful athletic programs can help brand a school as a winner. Quinnipiac and Valparaiso have scheduled Ivy League opponents to do just that. Schools as different as George Mason University, a state-funded commuter school outside of Washington, D.C.; Gonzaga University, a Jesuit school in Spokane, Washington; and the University of Connecticut have all artfully used success on the hardwood as a springboard to greater national prominence. Since 2000, Valparaiso, Butler University, and Belmont University all rode their Cinderella appearances in the NCAA Division I playoffs to celebrity.

But athletic scandals can infect the reputation of an entire institution. At St. Bonaventure University, in western New York, a flagrant athletic scandal incurred the well-deserved wrath of the NCAA and brought down the president of the university. Such violations of institutional integrity can be repaired, of course, but not quickly.

Brands, like the institutions they reflect, have a history and a future. Presidents and trustees can reinforce their institution's historic image, perpetuate it, reshape it to fit the times, and, of course, damage it through strategic mistakes and bad judgment. But they must understand the enduring qualities of the brand they inherit. They must pay attention to the history of their brand and to the durable institutional traditions it represents.

A BIT OF HISTORY

The marketing and branding of colleges and universities is the story of evolving institutional models: how creativity, persistence, and some luck combined to give historic brands new vitality. We look here at two types of American colleges: the small liberal arts college and the "comprehensive" small university with professional and graduate programs, the latter almost exclusively at the master's level.

Both types have deep roots in American higher education: the former is modeled on the elite liberal arts college; the latter incorporated professional and graduate programs into its curriculum to give it the appearance of a large, more diverse university. Indeed, most of the comprehensives have an undergraduate liberal arts program as well, which is, for many faculty members, the institution's real heart and soul.

Historically, both types marketed and branded themselves as liberal arts colleges. The comprehensive marketed its professional and graduate programs separately, and to an audience distinct from the recent high school graduates who entered as undergraduates. And for a while, that worked. But in the 1950s and 1960s, many state normal schools, which had been dedicated to preparing teachers, changed their designations to "university" and developed professional programs in business, health care, and other fields beyond education.

As public colleges and universities developed more professional programs, as well as master's degrees in education, business, and other applied fields, the Carnegie classification system introduced the label "comprehensive institution" in the 1970s. The new classification, along with competition from the lower-cost publics, presented a marketing and branding challenge for private colleges and universities. While the term "comprehensive" entered the academic lexicon, the word lacked both clarity and prestige in the mind of the education consumer, and thus had little appeal. Some colleges then found themselves in brand limbo. Clearly they were not pure liberal arts colleges, neither were they research universities. They were too career-oriented for those seeking a liberal arts degree, and too expensive for many working adults wanting professional education. They were at best indistinct, and at worst, "misfits."[7]

That perception persists. Members of the public, for the most part, understand the essences of liberal arts colleges and research universities. They are less clear on the roles of the so-called comprehensives. Thus, as a *type*, the comprehensive struggles to market its model of combined liberal arts and professional education and to gain recognition for its distinctive features. At the same time, the private comprehensives must persuade students that their offerings, which look much those vended by public schools, are in fact worth the difference in price.

BEGINNING THE TRANSFORMATION

Events of the 1970s and 1980s converged to threaten the survival of several solid, but largely undistinguished, schools. First, a marked downturn in numbers of traditional-age high school graduates jeopardized small liberal arts colleges, forcing them to cut costs and develop new programs as a survival strategy. Some, of course, did not survive, but many did institute curricular and marketing strategies that have resulted in dramatic enrollment growth and increased prestige and attention.

Second, the pure liberal arts degree began to lose its iconic status with an increasingly pragmatic public. As tales of graduates with literature degrees driving taxis abounded, more and more students demanded that their expensive college experience not only enlighten them but lead to a good job. That shift proved to be a marketing godsend for those colleges and universities that could tout an ability to add value to the education of their students by integrating liberal arts and professional program educational experiences.

Reaching New Markets

Seeing the handwriting on the wall, North Central College, Drury College (now Drury University), and the University of Redlands—among many others—added career and professionally oriented programs; opened evening and weekend programs and satellite campuses; adopted differential tuition strategies; and aggressively pursued adult and commuter students. Such nimble institutions enjoyed marketing success. Their enrollments and budgets grew during the 1980s, resulting in dramatic financial turnarounds that laid the foundation for further institutional transformation.

North Central, for example, grew from less than 800 students in the mid-1970s to 2,500 a decade later. Drury and Redlands grew even more—to approximately 4,000 students each.

Recently, riding the demographic growth of the traditional-age student market during the past decade, coupled with increasing competition from new storefront and online education purveyors, North Central and Redlands have successfully refocused their attention on the traditional-age student population and have experienced significant increases in undergraduate enrollment. It will be interesting to see how marketing strategies shift once again in the face of the decline in traditional-age students that some parts of the country will face during the coming decade.

A New Social Raison D'être

While entrepreneurial colleges and universities were finding ways to attune themselves to the more pragmatic interests of consumers, new social and educational ideas evolved to legitimate those developments. Ernest Boyer, president of the Carnegie Foundation for the Advancement of Teaching, launched a searching reexamination of higher education's mission and purposes during the 1980s. His work offered a transforming vision ideally suited to both emerging and established comprehensive institutions requiring or receptive to a turnaround. In a series of highly publicized studies, Boyer called for colleges to become more student-centered, to focus on core "common learning" experiences for all undergraduates, and to broaden notions of scholarship to include teaching and interdisciplinary and applied studies. Boyer advocated that colleges make student learning more powerful by linking theory and practice, and "thought and action," through closer relationships between students and faculty. He argued that colleges should become more powerful learning communities by connecting their academic and student affairs with their campuses and their communities. The Carnegie reports amounted to a social and educational philosophy that underpinned the work of entrepreneurial colleges and universities—hundreds of them attempting to adjust to new market realities.[8]

A Collaborative Approach to Meeting the Competition

Toward the end of the 1980s, deans and provosts from many colleges formed a study group to explore the identity, distinctive characteristics, and appropriate marketplaces for their comprehensive institutions. In addition to Boyer's ideas, they were also inspired by the thoughts of Frank Wong. Wong argued that the presence of both liberal arts and professional programs on their campuses, coupled with their commitment to teaching and general education, provided an opportunity to enhance student learning, especially by integrating liberal and professional studies. Integration, Wong proposed, would be a path to add value to student learning while serving both liberal learning and career goals.

Wong's ideas offered a distinct marketing advantage. Pure liberal arts colleges, he argued, lacked the professional programs that job-conscious students demanded. At the same time, research universities were too fragmented to respond to student needs for more personal attention. Due to their manageable size, the comprehensive institutions could turn the marketing challenges they faced into a unique niche that would serve both traditional-age and non-traditional-age students.

Wong helped to coin the branding notions that shaped the thinking and marketing practices of the deans and provosts in that working group. For example, he referred to the "disconnected specialization" of the research universities with their hosts of narrow, specialized majors and research emphases to contrast it with the "integrated" curriculum of the smaller comprehensives. He adopted the term "primary care professor" as a higher education analogy to the presumed antidote for a health care system in crisis.

If Boyer legitimized for a national audience the linkage of (1) liberal arts and career preparation and (2) scholarship with teaching, Wong shaped the thinking of the institutions themselves that would carry out the reformed educational program envisioned in Boyer's Carnegie reports.[9]

Sturdy American Hybrids

The finishing touches to the study group's work occurred in 1994 when Boyer called upon higher education to create new American colleges—in Boyer's mind, sturdy American hybrids that would renew traditions of service to society he associated with the colonial liberal arts college and with the land grant university system that originated with the 1862 Morrill Act.[10] Following up on the marketing of aligning American colleges with the public good, the study group called for the nation to rededicate itself to "taking values seriously; putting students first; and creating a nation of learners."[11]

At a famous conference held at Wingspread, Boyer urged American colleges to pursue an "integrative institution" strategy to leverage the multiple connections he had earlier articulated.[12] Alexander Astin, also present at the conference, and frequently in conversation with the study group, argued for a "talent development" measure of institutional excellence. He felt that excellence should fundamentally be determined by the value-adding outcomes of an institution's educational efforts, not by student selectivity at entrance or the magnitude of other measures such as endowment, number of library books, or faculty salaries.[13] His ideas were congenial to leaders at those nonelite institutions who felt they could produce results without all the expensive inputs of their better-branded competitors.

With the internal marketing analysis phase completed at the Wingspread conference, the Associated New American Colleges (ANAC) was established formally soon after in 1995, at a meeting of institutional leaders at the Carnegie Foundation offices in Princeton, New Jersey.

UGLY DUCKLINGS NO MORE

The ANAC experience demonstrates that effective marketing strategies grow out of core institutional values, an understanding of distinctive institutional strengths and opportunities, and a vision of student and societal benefit. Financial pressures and changing times forced institutions to think and behave differently, especially to become more attuned to the needs of the new, more pragmatic student mind-set. At the same time, the seminal work of Boyer, Astin, and Wong on higher education reform legitimated new entrepreneurial and market-focused strategies.

ANAC member marketing strategies have sought to express the comparative advantages of hybrid institutions that provide highly personalized education in small classes taught by faculty whose first commitment is to students. Those institutions offer a liberal arts experience in a residential campus community setting, combined with the diversity of students, faculty, programs, and opportunities associated with larger universities. Significantly, because they require a liberal arts core general education program of all undergraduates, they are able, with integrity, to offer major programs targeted to community needs, student career interests, and the desires of employers. Frequently, such programs combine classroom theory and significant student experience in a community of practice. Such universities have branded their products with language that resonates more effectively than the bland Carnegie "comprehensive" categorization.

Drury University, for example, branded itself as a "collegiate university," while the University of Redlands is a "liberal arts university." Elon University claims to combine the best qualities of neighboring Davidson College and Wake Forest University, blended with aspirations to achieve both a Phi Beta Kappa chapter and national professional accreditations. All ANAC member universities assert that they are regionally committed and nationally connected, as well as responsive to community needs.

Marketing the new American colleges has stimulated new messages under the heading of "integrative" branding. That approach introduces unexpected elements into the branding mix to contribute to a sense of distinctiveness. Ithaca College and Pacific Lutheran University, for example, are developing "sustainability" brands that emphasize and synthesize interdisciplinary, environmental, ethical, international, and community service program perspectives.

Many colleges are located in attractive, safe communities, but such locales can also be considered provincial, isolated, or boring. To overcome the negatives of campuses in, say, Springfield, Missouri, as Drury is, or almost anyplace in New York outside of Manhattan, such schools often underscore international learn-ing opportunities. Drury University has raised its "engaged community" profile through its "Global Perspectives 21" core program, which begins in a student's first year. It combines an interdisciplinary seminar, prominent speakers, and stu-dent life events all centered on compelling contemporary themes such as global sustainability, gender studies, and comparative cultural traditions.

Drake University, in Des Moines, brands itself as the "Gateway to the Globe" and backs its mission up with numerous international exchange programs involv-ing intensive language, cultural, and professional learning experiences. Arcadia University, located in Glenside, Pennsylvania, may push integrative branding to the limits. It offers "The Arcadia Promise: A distinctively global, integrative, and personal learning experience."

Hamline: The New American University

Hamline University, in St. Paul, Minnesota, faces acute, yet typical, challenges in marketing and branding its amalgam of liberal arts undergraduate study coupled with a law school and other professional programs. No institution in the state can match the University of Minnesota's array of first-rate professional programs. Neither is there a shortage of excellent liberal arts colleges in the region, includ-ing nearby Macalister College, ranked 24th nationally in the 2007 U.S. News & World Report liberal arts college ratings, and Carlton College, in Northfield, ranked 6th. Furthermore, Metropolitan State University, with centers throughout the Twin Cities and its suburbs, markets to older students at a price one-fourth of what Hamline charges.

Systematically, though, Hamline has met that competition—and flourished. It explicitly brands itself as "Hamline: The New American University." Inspired by a consultation with Boyer in the early 1990s, Hamline developed a comprehensive plan for institutional advancement with admissions, curricular, and fund-raising strands marketed via the ANAC paradigm. The Hamline board of trustees, which includes leading Minneapolis and St. Paul corporate CEOs, became deeply engaged in the planning process. (It is worth noting that 3M, Target, and Pillsbury are among the best-branded companies in America, and all have a strong presence in the Twin Cities.) As a result, the Hamline strategic plan reflects both corporate marketing expertise and the application of business processes to achieve high customer satisfaction and high cost-effectiveness.

That integration of educational philosophy with results-oriented business prac-tices culminated in a sophisticated marketing program, which emphasized that Hamline students would experience the best of liberal arts, professional studies, and community-based learning. Hamline made an additional commitment to high-quality learning outcomes as a sort of guarantee to its students. To deliver on its admissions promises, the Hamline curriculum was strengthened to provide interdisciplinary experiences, field applications of classroom work, and service opportunities in undergraduate and graduate programs across the institution, for example, internships, research, service learning, off-campus community projects, and study abroad.

Hamline's marketing has paid off handsomely in an enrollment increase of 25 percent in the past decade; a sesquicentennial fund-raising campaign that exceeded its $150 million goal; implementation of a capital construction and landscape master plan that has transformed the campus look and feel; and a "top ten" designation in the Universities-Master's (Midwest) category of the 2007 *U.S. News & World Report* rankings.

CORE NEW AMERICAN COLLEGE THEMES

All ANAC members anchor specific marketing messages in some version of the following core themes:

- Student-centered learning community featuring an engaged faculty and professional staff
- Programs that integrate liberal learning *and* career/professional preparation
- Education connecting classroom learning with community engagement for citizenship, career, and community development
- Affordability for all students; focus on cost-effectiveness and continuous improvement
- Value-centered, often church-related, campus culture

What follows are marketing and branding examples around those core themes.

Student-Centered and Engaged Learning Community

Elon University is an excellent example of successful marketing, billing itself as an engaged campus community focused on student learning. The "Elon Experiences"—experiential learning requirements of all undergraduates involving internships, leadership, service, and study abroad—have become a national curricular model, as well as a branding bonanza. Students play significant roles in the initiation and management of their Elon Experiences. Elon is known for its cocurricular transcript, which enables students to document their Elon Experiences as an important part of their professional resumes. Elon also emphasizes undergraduate research across the curriculum. Such innovations have had a significant marketing payoff in National Survey of Student Engagement results, which consistently place Elon in the top 10 percent of those surveyed in the category that describes the depth of student engagement in learning—on a par with the very best liberal arts colleges.[14]

Liberal Learning Plus Career Preparation

Acquiring the attributes of a well-educated person, as well as the skills to be a reasonably well-compensated one, are twin goals of all the new American colleges. Marketing career education and liberal learning seems to work when significant enrollment comes from the geographic region within a 50–100 mile radius of campus: where targeted marketing can reach its intended audiences; and where multiple media outlets exist to deliver specific program messages.

Such factors work in favor The Sage Colleges, located the capital region of New York (Albany, Troy, Schenectady). The Sage Colleges—comprising the Russell Sage College, in Troy; the Sage College of Albany; and the Sage Graduate School—offer career-specific programs for students seeking professional opportunities in the health professions, technology, and social service professions. The programs all have major internship, practicum, and applied project components, and all integrate liberal arts and professional preparation. Sage requires a strong general education program of all its undergraduates, which balances the career and professional tilt of most majors. The Sage Colleges also have aggressively positioned themselves to address gender issues and careers for women.

Quinnipiac University, whose turnaround experience is described more comprehensively in chapter 1, used a similar strategy of combining a liberal arts feel to the campus with strong career-oriented programs. It has more than doubled its enrollment since the mid-1980s. Quinnipiac also moved to a large campus near Hamden, Connecticut, where a lovely physical plant has been constructed in phases over the past two decades. Finally, taking advantage of its proximity to New York City, Quinnipiac has developed strong media and communications, law, social services, and health sciences programs.

Similarly, Belmont University, in Nashville, has developed the nation's largest college program in music business, a shrewd program strategy given its location. Nearly one-third of its undergraduate students major in music business, and a number of Belmont graduates are considered among the top 25 country music artists of recent years, which certainly helps recruiting. In addition, reflecting Nashville's status as a regional health center, Belmont has expanded its programs rapidly in the health professions, building two new academic buildings in the past three years. And it has developed a regional reputation for recruiting athletes with sterling academic records. Taken together, those steps have resulted in a 10 percent annual increase in students over the past five years, doubling enrollment in the last decade.

Many colleges and universities market their student cocurricular activities, but few link these noncredit experiences as closely to career preparation as do ANAC members. Collaboration between academic and student affairs is seen as a strategic imperative to maximize student learning outcomes and retention. Numerous student activities are highly organized with faculty advisers as a means for major programs to provide career-related practice and competition experiences. At North Central College, for example, many of the strongest majors sponsor activities such as Students in Free Enterprise, forensics, Model UN, and Moot Court to give students in fields such as business, communications, and political science well-developed skills in the practice of their fields of study.

Connecting Classroom Learning with Community Engagement

Wagner College, an institution operating with a thin financial margin, developed the "Wagner Plan"—a turnaround strategy designed to brand the college as a leader in preparing students to be socially committed citizens, as well as competent and ethical professionals. Coming at a time of repeated lapses at the highest corporate and political levels, the Wagner Plan has caught a wave of national publicity and acclaim, including a high-profile role in the Association of American Colleges and Universities civic engagement program, and the 2005 TIAA-CREF Hesburgh Award for outstanding educational innovation. The Wagner Plan has dimensions throughout all undergraduate years, requiring that all students link general education and major-program classroom learning with substantive internship and community service projects in corporations, nonprofit organizations, and government agencies. Although it is still too early to know to what extent the plan will result in enrollment increases, it has so far yielded some enrollment growth, a tenfold increase in endowment value, and highly visible brand recognition.

Numerous colleges have strengthened a socially progressive brand. Nearly a decade ago, for example, Mercer University, located in Macon, Georgia, announced a program to provide social and educational services to residents and to subsidize housing rehabilitation through low-interest mortgage loans to faculty who bought houses in a blighted neighborhood adjacent to campus. In cooperation with the university, local government officials and other opinion leaders are involved with the Mercer Community Development Center, which engages students and faculty in a variety of research and community development projects, school partnerships, and service learning projects.

The Sage Colleges entered into the University Heights partnership with the State of New York, the Albany College of Law, and another private institution to develop a 31-acre tract adjacent to the Sage College of Albany campus as a shared educational and commercial venture. In addition to providing income to Sage, the collaboration has resulted in expanded facilities and local economic development, access to important political and corporate leaders, and significant publicity and goodwill in the larger Albany region.

The University of Evansville and Butler University have received multimillion-dollar grants from the Lilly Endowment to engage faculty and students in entrepreneurship and business partnerships to help jump-start business development in economically challenged regions of Indiana, as well as to advance Lilly's initiative to encourage Indiana college graduates to stay in the state.

Affordability and Cost-Effectiveness

Many new American colleges must compete with flagship state universities and regional public comprehensives for students, and thus must face pricing and student aid challenges. Hamline, for example, charges about three times the tuition as the nearby University of Minnesota, and four times that of the regional state universities. Drury, in Springfield, Missouri, charges about twice what state residents would pay at the University of Missouri, whose main campus is much closer to the population centers of St. Louis and Kansas City. Relative to elite private colleges, however, most ANAC members have low-to-moderate tuition levels and offer substantial financial aid packages to assure diverse student bodies.

Significant marketing efforts are devoted to demonstrating that ANAC member colleges are affordable, and that even those who pay full tuition receive some subsidy. Still, communicating effectively that few students pay the full tuition, and that for many students the cost is comparable to state institutions, is tricky marketing.

The cost-effectiveness side of the equation relies heavily on the value-adding opportunities that small classes, experiential learning, and access to faculty provide. ANAC members make the case that those attributes make their price-premium worthwhile.

Value-Centered, Often Church-Related Institutions

Many American colleges have historic religious affiliations and emphasize core values, moral development, and ethical decision making and leadership consistent with the traditions of the mainline churches to which they are tied. Expressions of those values underscore a focus on students, the centrality of community, qualities of human relationships, and the interaction of learning with life and faith. A majority of ANAC-member students do indicate a religious affiliation, but the colleges welcome students of all, or no, religious persuasions.

Taglines tell the story of a values connection. Examples revealing church-relatedness include "University of Evansville—Civic Mission; Sacred Trust"; "The University of Scranton—A Jesuit University"; "Belmont University—Compassion, Intelligence, Courage, Faith"; and "Valparaiso University—Connecting Faith to Life." Such statements are designed to signal authentic connections to the denominational base of an institution while avoiding narrow sectarianism.

Hampton University, a midsize, comprehensive, historically black institution, emphasizes character development, self-discipline, and leadership—core values enforced through the honor code demanded of all students. The impact of the honor code in producing ethical leaders and professional integrity undergirds a remarkably successful appeal to talented and ambitious African American students. That integration of values, pragmatism, and service, and the presidential leadership of William R. Harvey, have enabled Hampton to raise some $275 million over the past decade, establish nationally accredited professional programs, undertake significant capital construction, and attract growing numbers of non–African American students.

LESSONS FROM THE UGLY DUCKLINGS

In addition to ANAC members, hundreds of other bachelor's and master's universities have transformed themselves through branding. Many of those institutions are members of the Association of American Colleges and Universities, the nation's leading higher education association championing liberal learning. The Council of Independent Colleges, a national association with a membership of more than six hundred mostly bachelor's and master's comprehensive colleges and universities, also advocates pragmatic educational outcomes. Some of the state-supported liberal arts colleges have affiliated themselves with the Council of Public Liberal Arts Colleges. Whatever their organizational affiliation, colleges that engage in branding and marketing have more success when they connect the ideas of such organizations with their own unique situations.

Several phases or stages are crucial to success. First must come a period of internal self-study to clarify identity, core values, and strengths, along with constituent aspirations and their relationship to institutional mission. Facilitators and consultants can help in stimulating candid discussions and bringing examples from elsewhere. But success in this first stage demands a brutally honest internal assessment. There are no panaceas or quick fixes.

Second, a college needs a marketing study that identifies connections between potential students and the institution's wares. That phase should proceed from the candid self-appraisal mentioned above. The colleges discussed in this chapter navigated that step with remarkable success, adding new programs that dramatically increased enrollment and attracted funds, media coverage, and higher rankings. One of the lessons learned is that communicating the quality of student experience and the learning outcomes a college provides makes for market appeal.

Third, a transformation must be internalized in the institutional culture of the college. As noted elsewhere in this book, successful turnarounds require internal transparency and buy-in from the campus community. Neither of those will occur if branding is considered as a cosmetic makeover to seduce students into enrolling. Aside from the damage that approach will cause to an institution's reputation for integrity, students will leave in droves if they do not experience what they were promised. In describing what makes for great branding, experts agree that "consistency in delivering on their promises" ranks at the top.[15]

NOTES

1. Frank F. Wong, *The Ugly Ducklings of Higher Education* (unpublished presentation, University of the Pacific, 1990).

2. James Twitchell, *Branded Nation: The Marketing of Megachurch, College, Inc., and Museumworld* (New York: Simon & Schuster, 2004), 134.

3. Ibid., 146.

4. Ibid.

5. Robert Frank, "Higher Education: The Ultimate Winner of Take-All Market," in *Forum Futures: Exploring the Future of Higher Education, 2000*, ed. Maureen Devlin and Joel Meyerson (San Francisco: Jossey-Bass, 2001), 4–5.

6. David Kirp, Elizabeth Popp Berman, Jeffrey T. Holman, Patrick Roberts, Debra Solomon, and Jonathan VanAntwerpen, *Shakespeare, Einstein, and the Bottom Line: The Marketing of Higher Education* (Cambridge, MA: Harvard University Press, 2004), 14.

7. "Turning an Overnight Success into a Lasting One," *New York Times*, April 2, 2006.

8. See, for example, Ernest L. Boyer, *Quest for Common Learning* (Stanford, CA: Carnegie Foundation for the Advancement of Teaching), 1981; *College: The Undergraduate Experience in America* (New York: HarperCollins, 1987); *Scholarship Reconsidered: Priorities of the Professoriate* (Stanford, CA: Carnegie Foundation for the Advancement of Teaching, 1990); and *Campus Life: In Search of Community* (Stanford, CA: Carnegie Foundation for Advancement of Teaching, 1990).

9. Frank F. Wong, "Primary Care Education: A New American College Model," *Perspectives: The New American College* 24 (Spring and Fall 1994): 15–35.

10. Cecil P. Staton, Jr., *A Sturdy American Hybrid: Associated New American Colleges, Member Institutions, and Distinctive Features* (Macon, GA: Mercer University Press, 2003), x–xi.

11. Wingspread Group on Higher Education, *American Imperative: Higher Expectations for Higher Education* (Racine, WI: Johnson Foundation), 1993, 7.

12. Ernest L. Boyer, "The New American College," *Perspectives: The New American College* 24 (Spring and Fall 1994): 6–12.

13. Alexander W. Astin, "Higher Education Reform and Citizenship: A Question of Values," *Perspectives: The New American College* 24 (Summer and Fall 1994): 79–91.

14. George Keller, *Transforming a College: The Story of a Little-Known College's Strategic Climb to National Distinction* (Baltimore: The Johns Hopkins University Press, 2004), 87.

15. Rita Clifton and John Simmons, *Brands and Branding* (Princeton, NJ: Bloomberg Press, 2003), 69.

CHAPTER

Academic Revitalization: Fulfilling the Turnaround Promise

Adrian Tinsley

DIFFERENT PATHS TO SUCCESS

After improving their finances, stabilizing enrollments, implementing new programs and marketing efforts, repairing or constructing new buildings, and increasing the confidence of leaders, faculty, students, and parents in their institutions, some institutions will rest on their well-deserved laurels.

For others at that point of self-congratulation—those that see genuine excellence as their goal—the hardest work still lies ahead, and they actively begin to implement Stage III. To those schools, survival or even improved reputation is not enough. They seek substantive change to the core educational mission and institutional culture. They want to analyze and improve the quality of their educational efforts, the relationships between faculty and students, and the attitudes of all members of the institutional community toward their work.

Unlike Stage II, Stage III looks inward. It works to revitalize the mission and culture of the institution. It seeks improvement in all programs and processes. In the context of a clear, strong vision for the future, senior leaders focus on changing internal beliefs, values, and interactions. Institution-wide conversations focus on creating the conditions for effective education. And all involved are open to feedback and to candid self-appraisal.

Stage III, then, is the stage where academic quality finally becomes real. For senior leaders, it requires the heaviest lifting of all. While trustees, presidents, and provosts must lead the work of academic revitalization, they cannot really drive it. Administrators cannot energize classrooms, libraries, and residence halls where the real learning happens. Presidents and provosts may—indeed must—insist on academic quality, but to get it, they must work through and with faculty and faculty governance structures, and they must encourage and reward faculty engagement in the process.

For senior leaders, Stage III is characterized by obsessive attention to improving virtually every dimension of institutional activity: from deciding whom to admit, what athletic conference to join, what courses and majors to offer, and what faculty to hire, to the kind of brick on new buildings and the color of campus plantings. The most successful Stage III schools are uncompromising in their commitment to focused change across the board.

This chapter discusses in detail the Stage III processes at three universities: the University of Denver, Northeastern University, and the College of New Jersey. Given their differences in location, size, type, and history, the three took dissimilar routes to similar destinations. By any measures they are outstanding examples of what perseverance and commitment to Stage III can yield.

The University of Denver Today

Founded in 1864, the University of Denver is the oldest independent higher education institution in the Rocky Mountain West. Carnegie-classified as "Doctoral/Research University—Extensive," DU currently enrolls some 9,500 students in professionally oriented undergraduate, master's, and doctoral programs, and in the liberal arts and sciences. Six percent of DU students are from outside the United States, and 54 percent of the student body is enrolled in graduate schools. The university fields 16 athletic teams in NCAA Division I.

Located within the City of Denver, DU enjoys a beautiful, architecturally consistent, well-maintained campus of 120 a cres. More than half of the campus's 67 buildings have been constructed in the last 15 years, and the replacement value of all the buildings is currently estimated at around $1 billion.

In its rankings for undergraduate education, *U.S. News & World Report* ranks DU within the top one hundred national doctoral universities. Target enrollment for undergraduate students is about 1,100 first-time, full-time, undergraduate students per year. Current students had an average high school GPA of 3.6 and an average SAT score of 1165 or an ACT score of 26. Forty percent of new undergraduate students come from Colorado, and 60 percent from out of state, with the heaviest draw from New England, the upper Midwest, California, and Texas. Freshman-to-sophomore retention rate is around 87 percent, while the six-year graduation rate hovers at 71 percent.

Undergraduate tuition (2005–06) is $27,756: 46 percent of first-year undergraduates receive need-based financial assistance. The discount rate (the average reduction from sticker price across all student payments) is 32 percent for first-year students and 29–30 percent overall. (According to the National Center for Education Statistics, the discount rate at the nation's most selective colleges is 27 percent.)

The College of New Jersey Today

Founded in 1855 as the New Jersey State Normal School, the College of New Jersey today is a high quality, public, primarily undergraduate residential college. Carnegie-classified as "Masters Colleges and Universities I," TCNJ comprises more than 50 professionally oriented and liberal arts/sciences programs in seven academic schools. Its current undergraduate enrollment is about 5,700 full-time undergraduate students and roughly 900 graduate students, 93 percent of whom are from New Jersey.

The college comprises 38 buildings on 289 landscaped and tree-lined acres in suburban Ewing, New Jersey, midway between Philadelphia and New York City. The buildings are Georgian; residence halls overlook a lake; and cars are confined to the campus perimeter. Twenty-one athletic teams compete in NCAA Division III.

Over the past 30 years, the College of New Jersey (the name was changed from Trenton State College in 1996) has pulled out of the pack and reinvented itself as New Jersey's public ivy. Target enrollment for undergraduate students is about 1,200 full-time students. Ninety-five percent of the freshman class ranked in the top fifth of their high school classes. SAT scores now average 1300 (for regularly admitted freshmen) and 1231 for all freshmen (including those granted admission under New Jersey's Equal Opportunity Fund program). Ninety-five percent of freshmen live on campus; the college guarantees two years of housing to all new, full-time, first-year students.

Tuition and fees (2005–06) are $9,856 for New Jersey residents, $15,820 for out-of-state students. Room and board adds $8,807, for a total cost of $18,663 (New Jersey) and $24,627 (out of state). Freshman-to-sophomore retention rate is about 95 percent, and the six-year graduation rate is 83 percent. In its "Best Universities—Master's" category, *U.S. News & World Report* has ranked the College of New Jersey tops in the Northeast among public colleges since 1993. *Barron's* lists TCNJ in its "Most Competitive" category (Princeton is the only other New Jersey school so listed).

Northeastern University Today

Founded in 1898 as a part-time night school, Northeastern University's campus today comprises 66 acres along Huntington Avenue in Boston, Massachusetts, and consists of 41 academic buildings and 28 dormitories and residential buildings. Its academic programs are clustered in schools and colleges, including a law school, a college of health sciences, and a college of business administration. *U.S News & World Report* ranks Northeastern as number one among universities that integrate classroom and real-world experiences and gives many of its schools and colleges top ratings for individual excellence.

Northeastern enrolls approximately 18,000 undergraduate students, 4,000 of whom are part-time; 600 law-school students; and an additional 2,700 graduate students, about half part-time. The undergraduate program at NU is five years, which includes significant paid co-op experience. In 2005, NU received 25,000 applications for 2,800 spots. Those who entered that fall had an average SAT score of 1260 or an ACT score of 26 as well as a high school GPA of 3.4. Freshman-to-sophomore retention stood at 83 percent in 2004.

Carnegie-classified as "Doctoral/Research University—Comprehensive," the university's tuition and fees vary across its programs, but the undergraduate tuition and fees for 2006–07 total approximately $17,000 per semester; room and board charges are approximately $5,000 per semester. Seventy-nine percent of entering freshmen receive financial aid. Northeastern draws primarily from the New England and the Mid-Atlantic regions, and approximately 5 percent of its undergraduate population is African American; 4 percent is Hispanic; and 6 percent is Asian. (The remainder is either Caucasian or of unknown ethnic origin.) Eight percent of NU's students are from outside the United States. Northeastern fields 19 NCAA Division I athletic teams.

ROUTES TO STAGE III

Dan Ritchie, a retired CEO of Westinghouse, became chancellor of the University of Denver in 1989, at the behest of fellow members of the university's board of trustees. At that time, the cumulative deficit stood at approximately $8 million, and by December, the operating deficit for FY 90 was projected at $1.4 million. Ritchie and the trustees knew from an earlier failed attempt to "fix" the university's budget that cutting was not the way to eliminate its continuing shortfalls. They needed to put the university on a completely different financial footing. When Jim Greisemer, Ritchie's new CFO, formerly the city manager of Aurora, Colorado, came on board in January 1990, even making payroll was doubtful. On Greisemer's first day on the job, the university attorney handed him the draft of a memo to close the college.

Neither Ritchie nor Greisemer had previous academic leadership experience, but both brought critical, relevant backgrounds: Ritchie in corporate management and finance, Greismer in the use of incentive systems to make people aware of the real costs of operation. With a doctorate from the University of Pennsylvania and many academic articles to his credit, Greisemer in particular was experienced in using financial systems to change people and organizations. But even though faculty and staff were desperate, they were highly skeptical of their new leaders' plans.

That skepticism evaporated within a year, when DU had broken even. Within two years, the university's colleges and departments had saved $2 million. With the crises averted, faculty and staff began to see what Dan Ritchie's leadership could mean to them, and Ritchie—who had meant only to fix the finances and stay "perhaps for a couple of years"—got interested in the university and its possibilities. Ultimately, he gave the University of Denver 16 years of smart, highly engaged, highly competent executive leadership. And in that time, the university moved from uncertain paydays to the academic revitalization of Stage III.

The University of Denver and Northeastern University both fought their way out of enrollment declines, stabilized their finances, rebuilt their physical plants, and set out to build the financial strength and faculty required to become nationally recognized private research universities—in crass terms, to make *U.S. News & World Report's* "Top 100" list. DU already had a solid regional reputation and a strong professional-school tradition. It needed to increase its resources, improve its research incentives, and attract a better graduate faculty.

Northeastern, however, faced very different problems. Like DU, but less dramatically, it was headed in the wrong direction. Payrolls were not in question, but freshman enrollment—after an 8 percent dip in the fall of 1989 and a 21 percent decline in the winter of 1990—plummeted another 28 percent in the fall of 1990.

The situation was not just a wake-up call for Jack Curry, the president, but a real crisis. He saw clearly that Northeastern had no choice but to take a different direction: to absorb the financial hit required to become a "smaller, leaner, better place to work and study—a place where academic excellence thrives through quality, not quantity."

Unlike the University of Denver, Northeastern's efforts required a genuine, though largely unpublicized, change of mission. Northeastern's roots and reputation were in offering regional opportunities: practical and applied programs to local, career-oriented students. Northeastern students got a job-market edge through the university's famous co-op work program, and—not insignificantly—co-op work paid their tuition costs. That model worked brilliantly before the rise of public higher education systems, and before the university's tuition and fees increased far beyond what students' part-time co-op work could cover. But it was no longer effective, and students were voting with their feet.

Under Curry's leadership, Northeastern capped freshman enrollment at 2,700 for all of 1991 and put a hiring freeze in place. Over three fiscal years, he cut $17 million from the budget, and eliminated 20 percent of the university's personnel— 700 employees in all—mostly, though not entirely, through attrition. But like the University of Denver, Northeastern could not cut its way out of its problems. Curry had to develop a new strategic direction for the university, and make sure it took hold.

Engaging faculty in the strategic planning process, Curry merged colleges; eliminated some programs, and added others; hired new faculty; revitalized the honors program; developed interdisciplinary studies; and instituted an international curriculum linked to studying abroad. He more than doubled Northeastern's endowment; ran a $225 million capital campaign; and began what became a multiyear effort to make the campus more residential. In 1991, Curry spent nearly half a million dollars on trees and grass—a risky strategy while employees were being laid off. But the turnaround efforts worked. By 1996, applications had increased from 10,000 to 13,000, SAT scores from 890 to 1055, and freshman-to-sophomore retention from 67 percent to 78 percent.

Like most public institutions, the College of New Jersey never had to deal with a near-death experience, not even, really, with declining enrollments. But in the 1970s—a period of declining enrollments nationwide—Trenton State's CFO Pete Mills saw that the numbers of college-age students were declining and realized what that could mean for the New Jersey state colleges, which (like most state colleges and universities at the time) were funded on an enrollment-based formula.

At the same time, Mills knew that even if the demographics turned upward again, Trenton State could not grow. Classrooms and laboratories were already stretched beyond their limits, and the state's funding system did not give him the ability to aggregate enough resources to catch up on maintenance, let alone construct new facilities for new students. The only way he could get control of Trenton State's finances and facilities would be to downsize. Not incidentally, downsizing could also permit the college to increase quality, and not just of the physical plant. Used correctly, downsizing could make a real difference to the quality of the college's entering students, and thus to its reputation.

By the spring of 1976, Mills had developed a financial model that could support downsizing and reduce the size of the freshman class. Mills sold the model and his downsizing plan to Clayton Brower, the president, and to the university's board of trustees. The incoming chair of the board, Erna Hoover, a graduate of Wellesley and Yale, knew what a high-quality liberal arts college could be. She saw the possibilities immediately and developed a passion for the proposition that "at least one state college should not cost what Princeton costs, and be available to the better students in New Jersey." Other members of the board were equally enthusiastic.

Even more important, however, Mills and Brower sold the downsizing concept and financial model to Ted Hollander, New Jersey's chancellor of higher education. Hollander agreed to let Trenton State keep 50 percent of the difference between the formula's projected appropriation and the number of freshmen enrolled. He even offered all the other New Jersey state college presidents the opportunity to downsize using Trenton State's model, but none embraced it, fearing the risk of reduced enrollments. (Ultimately, of course, all those schools' enrollments declined because of the demographic trends Pete Mills had anticipated.)

Today, Mills's "smaller but better" vision has been the guiding force for 30 years, under three successors, presidents, three separate configurations of state public higher education governance, and one name change.

Clayton Brower (1971–80) listened to a new CFO and took the downsizing risk. Harold Eickhoff (1980–99) embraced the vision of Trenton State as a residential liberal arts college in the public sector and made it his personal mission to attract better students. Eickhoff also built and rebuilt the campus to architectural consistency in the college's original Georgian style, pushed the name change from Trenton State College to the College of New Jersey through the board of trustees, and—most important to the college's long-term possibilities—won the intense political and bureaucratic battles that configured New Jersey public higher education in ways that permitted a public ivy to develop and thrive. Such consistent efforts over 25 years then put R. Barbara Gitenstein, who took office in 1999, in a position to develop academic programs and teaching pedagogies as good as the SAT scores, physical facilities, and landscaping the college now enjoyed.

Each of those presidents brought exactly the right qualities to lead the college meaningfully when he or she came on board. The board of trustees should receive considerable credit for that consistency of vision, and for choosing wisely, but still, the singleness of purpose at Trenton State/TCNJ is remarkable.

ESSENTIAL ELEMENTS OF ACADEMIC REVITALIZATION

Whatever its institutional type, a college needs three elements to successfully navigate Stage III revitalizations: the right leaders; the right model for institutional excellence; and the right choice of levers for change.

The Right Leaders

The right leaders are essential for one reason: Stage III transformation rarely begins anywhere but with a university's leadership. Although the College of New Jersey is a notable exception, academic revitalization is nearly always the result of passion and push from the president, the chief academic officer, or the board of trustees.

The University of Denver's efforts to improve the undergraduate experience began with the chancellor, and he and his chief academic officer pushed his ideas through a new planning process. Similarly, Northeastern's academic revitalization began with a beleaguered president who engaged and involved his faculty, both for educational purposes and to get their support.

As the cases indicate, neither autocratic leadership nor pragmatic problem solving can get the job done in Stage III. A president or chancellor has to be able to collaborate, to use institutional systems, processes, and players to encourage and motivate others to higher accomplishment. Yes, a CEO has to be able to sell the vision, but he or she must also be able to give and take effectively with the academic players, to listen, to modify positions in response to suggestions and complaints. Academic revitalization efforts are simply too broad and too complex to determine what's needed and to shepherd those solutions through the academic decision-making structures on one's own. Turnaround CEOs typically find at least one professional soul mate to think, plan, and partner with: a board chair, a CFO, or a CAO. In Stage III, because of the need for faculty buy-in, the partner most frequently is the CAO.

The Right Model for Excellence

A second precondition for success at Stage III is the right aspirational model for institutional excellence.

- The model for the College of New Jersey was clear by the late 1970s and has been consistent for more than 30 years: a small, public, residential liberal arts college offering challenging undergraduate programs and strong professional education.
- The model for the University of Denver emerged more slowly from the size and strength of its professional programs and from the chancellor's interest in what he saw as higher education's inadequacies in undergraduate education. From those two points of pressure, DU began to aspire to become a small private research university of the highest quality, to crack the "Top 100" list, but with special focus on talent development for undergraduate students through active and experiential learning.

- Under Jack Curry, Northeastern University looked to fewer but better students on a more residential, more attractive campus: new buildings, trees, and grass for its urban setting. His successor, Richard Freeland, built on that toward Northeastern's current mission: to be a "national, research university that is student-centered, practice-oriented, and urban."

Whatever model an institution chooses, it must be realistic. The improving college or university must be have, or be able to acquire, what it needs to meet its goals. Some at Bridgewater State College in Massachusetts, for example, hoped the college could become a public ivy, but the institution didn't have the wherewithal: the constraints of the Massachusetts State College Building Authority made acquiring the necessary residential capacity an unrealistic goal. Given its location and the region's needs, Bridgewater chose the model it could more realistically attain: a higher-quality regional comprehensive.

Green Mountain College's location in rural Vermont constrained it from growing much bigger in size, but it learned to capitalize on its isolation through an environmental curriculum and active participation in the national "Eco League" of environmental schools. Lasell College, in a pricey suburban residential area outside Boston, was able to expand from two-year to four-year programs and from single-sex to co-ed because its location and residence-hall capacity could attract the traditional-age students the new mission required. The University of Connecticut had half a dozen political insiders who knew Connecticut politics cold and had the legislative connections necessary to get the resources to put UConn on the road to becoming—as the mission statement says—"a great state university."

THE RIGHT LEVERS FOR CHANGE

The third requirement for Stage III success is to choose the right tactics, that is, select the right levers. In Stage III, leaders look hard at all the variables they can use to push an institution toward becoming what says it wants to be. National and regional rankings; size; quality of students and faculty; degrees and programs offered; organizational systems and structures; resource acquisition and deployment; athletics; and cocurricular programs—all are up for examination.

National and Regional Rankings

Most colleges and universities in Stage III transformation pay close attention to their standings in a variety of national and regional rankings and ratings, and particularly to those of *U.S. News & World Report*. For better or worse, the magazine's rankings have become an integral part of American higher education. Students, parents, donors, boards, and communities are always eager to know how their institution rates each year. Thus an institutional goal to move up in the rankings—even to break into a new rankings category—is nearly de rigueur.

The University of Denver, for example, wanted to become a nationally renowned private research university with a focus on developing undergraduate talent. By 2007, *U.S. News & World Report* ranked DU 88th for undergraduate education among doctoral universities and also ranked its schools of law and social work among the top 100 in their categories. The *Wall Street Journal* ranked DU's Daniels College of Business among top undergraduate business programs: fourth for high ethical standards, and eighth among other regional business schools.

Among 165 colleges and universities in the Northeast, *U.S. News & World Report* ranks the College of New Jersey fifth on its 2007 list of best "Universities-Master's (North)." (TCNJ is the only public institution to appear in the top ten.) Attaining that ranking was integral to President R. Barbara Gitenstein's academic transformation strategy for TCNJ.

Under President Richard Freeland's leadership, Northeastern University set the goal of becoming one of *U.S. News & World Report's* "National Universities: Top Schools," while continuing to emphasize its urban mission and focus. Toward that goal, the university made a number of specific improvements to elevate its rank among its peers—for example, lowering the sizes of as many classes as possible to fewer than 20 students, which is one of the magazine's quality indicators.

In addition, Northeastern measured itself against a number of its competitors—institutions with comparable enrollment and academic profiles. Each year, President Richard Freeland and Northeastern's trustees looked at a report card with dozens of criteria that ranked Northeastern with other comparable universities on measures related to student selectivity, student success, institutional resources, and academic reputation. Northeastern took the old saw "What gets measured gets better" literally, and made a very thorough job of it, using the broadest set of the possible levers for change. In 2007, the *U.S. News & World Report* rankings had Northeastern at number 98 in the "National Universities: Top Schools" category.

External ratings, however, are more than public relations tools to attract students or to please a university's wider constituencies. They also help parents, faculty, and staff understand what a university cares about and how resources for improvement are likely to be deployed. Almost universally, then, Stage III institutions give real time and attention to the process of identifying the appropriate external rankings, using them as one tool for setting institutional improvement goals and directing attention and resources to the activities that will help them improve their overall quality.

Getting Better Students

When colleges and universities undertake a turnaround, they typically begin with efforts to improve the academic quality of their undergraduate students. Strategic decisions about rightsizing for financial strength and facilities utilization come first. But within those parameters, most institutions then decide to downsize: to cut off the bottom of the applicant pool and recruit for better academic qualifications at the top. That strategy usually works, though it's seldom easy. Taking fewer first-year students requires serious financial planning, including smart decisions about acceptable discount rates. Higher test scores among incoming students mean better efforts at branding, marketing, and—most important—more shoe leather on the recruiting road.

The College of New Jersey learned those lessons the hard way. In 1975, freshmen entering Trenton State had mean SAT scores of 890 and a class rank of 73 percent. It took a full decade to raise the SATs to 1015 and the class rank to 77 percent. President Harold Eickoff visited every high school in New Jersey during his first five years as president, literally signing up students one by one. But his efforts gathered momentum. By the mid-1990s Trenton State's SAT scores (for regular admits) had crossed the 1200 mark. In 2004 they reached 1300. Today, TCNJ gets nearly 6,500 applications for 1,200 places in the freshman class and admits fewer than half of those who apply.

Most colleges and universities take that path to student quality. At one time, Northeastern was dipping very low into its applicant pool, accepting 94 percent of applying students. Even so, between 1989 and 1990, freshman enrollment fell from 3,833 to 2,730, triggering President Curry's decision to lead Northeastern onto the "smaller, leaner, better" path. In the fall of 2005, the university received 28,000 applications for 2,500 spots; and the mean high school GPA of admitted students was 3.55.

Chancellor Dan Ritchie also sought better undergraduate students for the University of Denver, but Ritchie took a contrary approach. A man who trusted his own judgment, he was not much interested in high SAT scores or application essays: the former didn't measure motivation or character, he felt, while a consultant or parent might have shaped the latter. Ritchie cared about a student's personal characteristics: good character; high motivation to learn; and an open mind. Ritchie had visited what he describes as "the best business school in India" and learned that it annually conducted 10,000 interviews to select 300 students for the first-year class. He asked the DU staff, "Why can't we do that?"

Not everyone thought it was a great idea—or even a good one—but Ritchie listened to concerns, made modifications, and then insisted. Now, at 32 sites around the United States, every undergraduate applicant to the University of Denver undergoes a twenty-minute structured interview by a team that includes at least one DU graduate and one member of the faculty or staff. The questions are emphatically not for "getting to know you" purposes. They are instead standardized and pilot-tested to probe motivation to learn; integrity and honesty; and openness to difference and new ideas. Currently DU budgets $400,000 annually for the program, which includes one full-time staff member and the travel and on-site costs for admissions staff and volunteer interviewers.

Does it make a difference to student quality? In terms of actual admissions decisions, only on the margins. "Mostly," one admissions staff member says, "it doesn't change our initial impression, but it makes a huge difference to about 50 students we interview. They're not all admits, either. We've denied some 4.0 students on the basis of the interview: they're not motivated to learn, or they're dishonest, and they tell us so."

The interviews do help to identify the "motivated and engaged kids"; to choose wisely "among the disadvantaged kids"; and to sell prospective DU students on the "personal interest DU will take in them if they matriculate," according to a recruiter. DU's development professionals laud the program: the interviews engage young graduates with the institution, which is likely to translate into later gifts. And faculty who participate see the interviews as a way to have a hand in shaping the classes they'll be teaching.

Finally, the interview process is interesting because it positions DU as one of the few American colleges that seeks, both in policy and practice, to disconnect a drive for higher test scores from a desire for higher academic quality.

Stronger Academic Programs

As the cases demonstrate, in Stage III transformations, better students usually come before stronger academic programs. The reason is obvious: trustees and senior administrative leaders can control student recruitment and admissions procedures and can decide upon and implement changes in those areas. But academic programs are designed, approved, taught, and evaluated by faculty. Thus academic improvement is longer and more complex than administrative improvement. Happily, when faculty see that the quality of their students is improving, they usually wish to make their programs and courses more challenging.

The College of New Jersey

At the College of New Jersey, it was faculty who decided to make a serious push for academic transformation. In the words of the president of the faculty senate, faculty were "embarrassed" that the quality of the educational offerings had not kept pace with the quality of the college's students. They were ready for a leader who could develop and strengthen the academic decision-making system as a precursor to improving academic quality. They took their concerns to the board and convinced its members to make a change in president.

When the board chose R. Barbara Gitenstein as the new president, the faculty responded by delivering to her a position paper, "The Ten Big Issues Confronting TCNJ." It called for sweeping changes to TCNJ's consultation and decision-making processes, governance structure, and planning processes. Faculty also asked for changes to the college's library and information management systems; the use and support of adjunct faculty; and—most important to academic transformation that followed—changes to the pedagogies that supported student learning at TCNJ. In other words, Gitenstein and her provost, Steve Briggs (who arrived a year later), had the enormous benefits of coming to a college with strong, positive faculty leadership and receiving a real mandate for radical change.

Because the faculty was ready, Gitenstein and Briggs were able to move quite quickly into Stage III. By the end of her first year, Gitenstein had collaborated with faculty leaders to reinvigorate and strengthen the college's governance system. By the end of her second year, she and Briggs had begun to determine how to provide stronger intellectual experience for students. They wanted more internships and experiential learning, more undergraduate research, more study abroad, and more Fulbrights, Goldwaters, and Trumans. And they didn't want add-ons, but one-on-one or small-group learning experiences embedded in the college's academic core.

The only way to accomplish those goals, Briggs thought, was to "reset the system": to require all faculty to rethink pedagogies, programs, and courses all at once. His responsibility, then, was to figure out the economics of the process and to develop the carrots and sticks. Perhaps faculty members—part of a system-wide, nine-campus faculty union—could teach three course units, rather than the required four, but be required to document the additional unit of work. That could be the carrot. Nothing in New Jersey law or executive-office policy pro-hibited such a change; neither did the stipulations of the collective bargaining agreement. The challenge was to make the economics of the course-reduction plan work. By the end of Briggs's first year on the job, he announced the academic transformation process.

By the end of the next year—year one of the academic transformation process—he had a model under discussion and economic scenarios that could work. In the second year, design work began on the majors and the liberal studies (general education) program. "We just said to the departments, 'See if you can do this'—we did it that simply," Briggs said. Faculty looked to schools such as Swarthmore College, Williams College, Amherst College, and Colgate University for their program models.

At the beginning of the third year, course revisions began. Each and every course had to be revised. New courses "had to be used to consolidate and extend learning—not to input information." And because there were fewer courses, each new course had to be demonstrably more demanding than its original. A lot of jawboning was required, as well as a firm hand. But the governance system was ready to handle the process, which was critical to the success of the effort.

Not every course had been revised by the beginning of the fourth year, but amazingly, the new curriculum was ready overall for implementation. There were problems, of course, but according to Briggs, "It all worked surprisingly smoothly." The faculty got the carrot—the three-course teaching load. And TCNJ got a genuinely better educational experience for its students: the study groups, the undergraduate research projects, and the more-demanding courses.

The University of Denver

At both the University of Denver and Northeastern University, the push for academic revitalization came first from the chief executive—as one of a num-ber of turnaround strategies. Both universities were experiencing highly visible enrollment declines; Northeastern's freshman enrollments were plummeting, and DU's financial shortfalls had prompted thoughts of closing completely. At both universities, CEOs worked hard to engage their faculty through speeches, strategic planning processes, departmental visits, one-on-one's with faculty leaders, and give-and-take with the faculty governance system. In DU's case, a very effective chief financial officer designed financial incentives that could help encourage change, but the president and the provost led academic transformation.

Chancellor Dan Ritchie had a strong personal interest in undergraduate edu-cation. Though he had enjoyed his undergraduate years at Harvard, his business experience, reading, and travel had all led him to believe that the experience undergraduates currently get at most American universities is neither very useful nor very interesting. Ritchie believed quite strongly in hands-on learning for undergraduate students: not just lectures and tests, but team projects, joint faculty-student research projects, leadership opportunities, study abroad—whatever could connect book-learning with an individual student's own experience. Even field trips could be enriching. Though Ritchie never used the phrase, he wanted undergraduates to have the opportunity for *engaged learning* at the University of Denver.

Early in his chancellorship, Ritchie appointed Bill Zarenka, who was DU's dean of arts and sciences, as an internal provost and asked him to design a planning process that could involve DU faculty in developing a new mission statement. Together, they created the University Planning and Assessment Committee (UPAC), which included some trustees but was weighted toward faculty.

That group determined a simple mission for the University of Denver: to provide education of the highest quality. The chancellor and his immediate staff, however, were the first among equals when it came to defining that broad statement. Of course DU's goals emphasized scholarship, research, and creative activity, but they also stressed "fostering values"; undergraduate distinctiveness; a global perspective; diversity; talent development for both students and staff; rigorous self-assessment; university involvement in the community; and responsible management.

UPAC held the discussions; Zarenka drafted the documents; and Ritchie and Zarenka lobbied for them with members of the faculty senate and through personal visits to every department and unit at DU. In reality, Ritchie spent a year listening to DU's faculty and staff and sharing with them his sense of what DU could become; what the possibilities for the university really were; and where they might personally develop new initiatives and connect them with the university's new direction.

Over 16 years, Ritchie accomplished most of what he set out to do: the interview process he thought so important, for example. And the Cherrington Global Scholars Program, which now offers qualified DU undergraduates the opportunity to study abroad for a quarter or semester at no cost beyond what the student would pay to DU. "Writing Across the Curriculum" and "Quantitative Reasoning/Applied Math Through the Disciplines" programs have been installed. First-year undergraduate students are now required to bring laptops to campus. Most recently, the Marsico Initiative, a $10 million gift from a DU alumni couple, has funded new undergraduate curriculum improvements. UPAC oversaw all those improvements and continues to guide new academic initiatives.

Northeastern University

Though not publicly announced as such, Northeastern's new strategic direction required nothing less than a genuine institution-wide mission and culture change. If Northeastern could no longer thrive as an "opportunity college" for local students hoping to support their education through earnings from co-op placements, if Northeastern wanted fewer, better students, then the academic programs would have to change as well.

President Curry probably engaged Northeastern's faculty in the university's strategic planning process as much for buy-in as to develop its content, but the results were impressive. Two hundred faculty members in 18 separate work groups helped to cut $17 million from the academic budget over three fiscal years. At the same time, 27 new academic programs were added, a new model for general education was created, and the honors program was revitalized—from 150 participants in 1989 to 1,250 in 1996. New faculty hires were made; interdisciplinary studies were emphasized; and study abroad was expanded. The university established a research development fund that reached $32 million by 1996, and engaged 25 percent of the faculty. All that effort was designed to make Northeastern more attractive to those fewer, better students it was now determined to serve. And the changes happened quickly, jump-started by the enrollment crisis.

One of the most interesting things about Northeastern's turnaround is that it was conceived and led by an insider. Jack Curry had spent his entire career at Northeastern, and yet he could see clearly that the university would have to become an entirely different kind of place. He represents an unusual example of an insider who could rise to the task of leading a Stage III turnaround.

Better Faculty for Better Students

Since the early 1990s, the large faculty cohort that began teaching in the '60s and '70s has been retiring, permitting most higher education institutions to make new faculty hires. In a buyer's job market, colleges and universities have been able to raise the bar for new tenure-track faculty: the right terminal degree is now uniformly required, preferably from the "right" institution. And new faculty members are expected to have a research program already in progress—and if that program has already produced results, so much the better. But even given an excellent pool in which to fish, colleges and universities cannot improve faculty quality on the cheap.

That means that colleges and universities seeking better faculty will be making resource deployment decisions on two fronts: the number and quality of new tenure-track full-time hires; and the ratio of new full-time hires to the part-time "at will" faculty now doing more and more of the routine undergraduate teaching work. For Stage III quality, the choices will be made within the parameters of the model to which the institution aspires.

Northeastern and the University of Denver, for example, are both seeking "Top 100" research university status. They will thus try to match faculty salaries and will research start-up incentives and full-time to part-time faculty ratios to those of their research-extensive competitors. The College of New Jersey will seek faculty on the leading edge of their disciplines who are also committed to interaction with undergraduate students. Each of the schools will measure their faculty ratios and class sizes against their competition, looking most closely at the numbers that affect rankings in *U.S. News & World Report*.

Chief academic officers and chief financial officers are accustomed to considering modeling and costing a variety of scenarios for hiring faculty but rarely think systematically about faculty development. Like other professionals, faculty need time to reflect on their own teaching and research performance; colleges and universities need to provide the structures that demand that they do so. Traditional faculty development opportunities (sabbatical leaves, research support, conference travel, even most teaching and learning centers) are accessed by individual faculty members at their own initiative, for their own research or teaching-development projects. Funds for those purposes, however—while hugely important to individual faculty members who benefit from them—rarely have an institution-wide impact on academic quality.

At Stage III, new kinds of institutional efforts are needed. Groups of faculty must work together to develop new or improved academic programs, new teaching-learning models, and new ways of measuring success. That sort of work is rarely successful when given over to elected or appointed "volunteers" on top of their normal teaching and research responsibilities. Like the other elements of academic revitalization, it requires leadership, time lines, focused resources, and accountability. It needs direction from the top, as well as incentives: course reductions during term time, perhaps; money for workshops or conferences; or team participation in national endeavors. It needs benchmarks and progress reports and metrics for measuring success.

Indeed, few institutions define their goals for professional development expenditures, while fewer still track expenditures across many purposes, projects, and categories to analyze how—or even whether—they contribute to institutional improvement. Were they to make such analyses, senior leaders would likely get an unpleasant surprise: that the expenditures are less than 1 percent of their operating budget, and that they are untargeted and unfocused.

When expenditure targets are set, and development funds linked to specific institutional needs, academic transformation comes more quickly. At the College of New Jersey, comprehensive Stage III transformation took four years from conception to the first year of implementation, and by higher education standards that was fast. But TCNJ got it right: those four years genuinely improved the college's academics, creating better programs and courses, better learning opportunities for students, and—not incidentally—a better faculty for the College of New Jersey.

Measuring Progress

Faculty may not usually lead the work of academic revitalization, but faculty members always drive it. Teaching and learning really do get better one course, one faculty member at a time. And trustees, presidents, and provosts can help faculty use some of the newer performance measurement tools effectively.

For overall institutional performance, particularly in desired incremental improvements, benchmarking is still the most powerful tool. Nothing focuses the mind more sharply than comparisons: how are we doing versus the competition? the institutions we think we're better than? the institutions we are striving to become? Northeastern, as noted earlier in this chapter, makes a very thorough job of benchmarking and reporting annually on literally scores of variables related to mission, goals, faculty, students, and management. Over time, incremental changes add up.

The twenty-year-old assessment movement provides a second set of tools that can be helpful in Stage III. All regional accrediting associations and most state governments (for public colleges and universities) now demand documentation of academic program outcomes, retention and graduation rates, student learning outcomes, outcomes for graduates, and student satisfaction. *Measuring Up*, the annual report card from the National Center for Public Policy and Higher Education, is making initial efforts to measure learning outcomes across states. Slowly and painfully, typically after contentious debate and methodological argument, most colleges and universities have learned how to generate such data, and Stage III leaders can use them.

The National Center for Education Statistics, a unit of the U.S. Department of Education, publishes statistics that can be extremely valuable to institutions in a Stage III turnaround. Its Integrated Postsecondary Education Data System (IPEDS), available at http://nces.ed.gov/ipeds, presents data from a series of surveys that collects institution-level data about enrollments, faculty salaries, finances, and program completions, among other information. It allows an institution to compare itself to other institutions on variables the institution itself can select. An institution can choose its own group of peers or can allow IPEDS to identify like institutions. If, for instance, a college wants to see how its admissions criteria or financial aid structures stack up against those of its competitors—or to those colleges it is seeking to emulate—it can generate a spreadsheet that will make the comparisons obvious.

Nationally normed faculty and student satisfaction measures can also be quite useful in Stage III improvement efforts, even though they cannot directly measure teaching quality or learning outcomes. The Noel-Levitz Student Satisfaction Inventory, for example, is widely used. The National Survey of Student Engagement (NSSE) has developed a way to measure and compare a school's educational performance on five standards related to helping students learn: the level of academic challenge; active and collaborative learning; interaction among students and faculty members; enriching educational experiences; and a supportive campus climate.

SUMMARY AND LESSONS LEARNED

What do we know about the requirements for successful Stage III transformation? for academic revitalization? for transformative change to the quality of the educational effort at the college or university core?

We know that improvements at Stage III are hard, but they are not mysterious. Success requires clear definition on the front end, laser-beam focus, and hard, persistent work over time—efforts not from the few, but by the many. That work cannot happen without leadership, but it is by no means the responsibility of leaders alone. It must occur at all levels of the institution, and particularly among the faculty. As the stories of this chapter show us, the principles that lead to success in Stage III are clear:

- **Excellence is everyone's goal.** An institution must choose *the right excellence model*, must ask and answer the right questions. What type of school do we aspire to be? At what stage are we? What's the next level for us? What distinguishes us from like institutions? Why are we important? Beyond surviving, beyond sustaining and advancing our institution, do we have a higher purpose?

- **Leadership counts.** The right trustee leadership and the right CEO must be in place, and they must have the right working relationships. Autocrats can't lead a Stage III process; neither can technical problem solvers. Stage III leaders drive the transformation process but mostly work through others. A CEO needs vision, passion, and obsessive commitment, but also strong communication and collaborative and team-building skills. And of course, a CEO needs the right team and the right chief academic officer. That CAO will be the critical player in Stage III: ensuring that new programs, pedagogies, and processes are developed and funded, and pushing them with—and through—faculty and institutional structures to reality.

  Trustees must commit themselves to understanding the process of academic revitalization. They must expect intelligible and cost-effective plans from university executives, and they must listen carefully to any relevant constituencies that oppose those plans. And, most importantly, once trustees have approved a strategy, they must support the university officials who are carrying it out.

- A **functional governance system** is a necessity, both internally and—for public colleges and universities—externally.

  Stage I and Stage II decisions can be made and implemented by a president and board without consultation with faculty, but the core internal changes required by Stage III cannot. The kind of governance system—a college assembly, a faculty senate, a union—is not important, but the system has to be viewed as legitimate by those who use it, and it has to work. Many of higher education's consultation and academic decision-making systems, unfortunately, do not. They are old, designed for an earlier era, and suffering from executive neglect.

  In the public sector, where legislators and state governance systems control missions, physical facilities, funding, academic programs, and most significant academic and financial policies, the external governance layer is more critical to Stage III success than the internal—and very much harder to deal with. Northeastern and the University of Denver both did impressive work, but it was child's play compared to what Trenton State College had to accomplish in order to become the College of New Jersey. Carefully cultivated political support for two successive major changes to higher education governance created conditions in the state that made TCNJ's success possible. Without those conditions, the transformation simply could not have happened.

- **Resources matter.** Yes, people count more than dollars when a school is at Stage III, but improving the core—educational programs, pedagogies, and processes—takes money. A Stage III school will likely need money for new faculty who can help develop and push an agenda for excellence. It will certainly need dollars for structures (e.g., teaching and learning centers), program development (e.g., retreats, seminars, workshops, national meetings), and measurement efforts (e.g., program evaluation, learning outcomes assessment). Both faculty and senior leaders will need to strengthen institutional visibility on the national scene by presenting at conferences and participating in national projects.

- **Even transformational change is incremental,** and in the end the keys to success are simple: choosing *the right levers for change* and developing the *discipline to measure progress every single year.* What gets measured gets better, so there's nothing more important than choosing what to measure. After resources, what are the priorities? Better physical plant? More students? Better students? Better faculty? D-I athletics? Better endowment? More community interaction? Better technology? All at once? One at a time? In which order? Boards of trustees and CEOs are responsible for making sure that choices among priorities are correct and clear. It's a CEO's responsibility to insist that measurement tools are appropriate, and to see that senior leaders, along with members of the board, get usable progress reports every year.

We see then, that while financial resources are important, they cannot guarantee institutional transformation. In the end, only four things really count: the right leadership; that leadership's ability to choose, sharpen, and sell the right vision; internal and external conditions that permit (or can be made to permit) an institution to work toward the vision incrementally and over time; and finally, focus, persistence, and attention to detail—very hard work for as long as it takes. Those four together open the doors to the possibility of a Stage III turnaround. Without any one of them, the doors remain closed.

SECTION II

Special Topics

CHAPTER 5

A Practical Guide to Financial Matters

Michael T. Townsley

Orchestrating the financial turnaround of a private college is more than fund-raising, finding new students, and firing the chief financial officer—or hiring a new one. A financial turnaround requires systematic, long-term focus—a difficult task for a president who has been spending every spare moment seeking gifts and endowments to staunch acute financial hemorrhages. That quest is a losing proposition, however. Even if some holes are plugged, new deficits spring out elsewhere—and elsewhere still—until the financial structure of the college collapses, the green finally flowing into the red.

Since 2000, many private colleges have found themselves financially challenged by a disorderly stock market and changing accounting practices. The market crashes of 2000 and 2001 resulted in a string of deficits, thanks in part to real losses of gifts and endowment draws—deficits that were compounded, at least on paper, by new accounting standards that required reporting of unrealized losses on annual financial statements.

While the market has since stabilized, it remains 8 percent below its 2000 high, and other problems exist. Endowment draws still don't produce enough funds to keep pace with inflation. Budgets have felt the sting of recent explosive increases in fuel costs. Demographic data suggest that many private institutions will see their student markets begin to shrink dramatically in 2008. Presidents who expect to manage those crises must look deeply into their budgets, student markets, and competitors' retention strategies—and most importantly, as described in this chapter, *employ a sound financial management model that uses a set of accepted diagnostic, strategic, and reporting tools* to

- know the precise financial condition of the institution;
- design a financial strategy that builds on strengths and eliminates weaknesses;
- track performance, identify problems, and change what must be modified; and
- keep the president and board informed about strategic financial performance.

This chapter is divided into four sections: diagnostic tools, which deals with accepted methods for analyzing financial performance; the strategic turnaround development stage, which employs the diagnostic tools to identify where to focus action; strategic performance monitoring, which describes how to monitor strategic plans; and strategic comments, which offers several important considerations about turnaround strategies.

CASE STUDY: SECTION ONE

Rubicon College (a fictitious amalgam of numerous institutions going through a financial turnaround), a liberal arts college on the East Coast, has a checkered past. Founded as an academy for wayward seminarians in 1815, it closed its doors in 1901, then again in 1922, 1933, and at the start of World War II. After the war, it reopened as a four-year technical college. From the 1980s until 1993, Rubicon offered career-oriented bachelor and master's degrees to its yearly enrollment of 350 to 375 students.

In 1993, a new president gave enrollment a kick start, jumping it to 975 students by 1998. She was also a whiz at capital campaigns; she created an endowment fund for the first time by obtaining a $28 million gift, and she obtained 40 percent of the cost of four new buildings. Rubicon, through her leadership, was becoming a first-class institution. Then the unexpected happened: she left Rubicon in early 1999 to lead a prestigious university in Chicago.

That unexpected turn of events shattered the hopes of everyone at the college, especially those on the board of trustees. Their shock quickly turned into an internal power struggle, because powerful board members, who had all played on Rubicon's acclaimed football teams of the 1960s, had not approved of all the changes made by the president. They delayed appointing a new president so that they could rotate the presidency among themselves. Soon, any hope of turning the college into a first-class institution turned to ashes as plans stalled, enrollment shrank, and gifts dried up. The power struggle finally ended after four years with their resignation. Within a year a new president was named.

By the time the new president arrived in 2003, the college was in dire straits: enrollment was down to 825 students, the endowment fund was gone, deficits were commonplace, and there was barely enough cash on hand to buy paper clips. Moreover, bondholders had notified the college that the balance due on the bonds would be called for payment, if the college did not turn around in a year.

The big question at the time was what the new president would do: close the college, merge it, or continue its long history of limping from one financial crisis to another. The road that the new president took to develop a strategic plan for a financially stable college provides many valuable lessons to anyone planning a financial turnaround.

DIAGNOSTIC TOOLS

Before a financial strategy can take shape, a president must know the true financial condition of the institution. Guesses, rumors, or expectations built on hope or good intentions won't work. Empirical tools such as ratio, trend, and marginal analysis have become accepted methods for discovering financial weaknesses and strengths to building a workable financial turnaround strategy.

After trend, marginal, or ratio analysis identifies a discrepancy, the relevant ratio or financial component must be deconstructed to define the problems, and to guide development of a strategic plan to deal with problems, for example, slow collections on student bills, or to address the major increases in financial aid associated with major declines in enrollment.

A college's diagnostic tools should focus on major financial drivers of the institution, those that govern the flow of funds into, through, and from the institution. Examples include enrollment, matriculation yields, net tuition, compensation, plant, cash flow, investments, debt, or net assets. Their location and impact on finances depends upon a college's unique financial structure and on whether it is public or private.

The remainder of this section describes the diagnostic tools and concludes with a four-stage model that uses those tools to diagnose the financial condition of the institution.

Trend Tables

Multiyear trend tables allow a longer-term view of changes in dollars or ratios. While simple eyeball comparisons at one point in time are useful, computing simple and compound rates of change results in invaluable projection tools. For example, if a comparison of total revenue and expense growth rates reveals that expense rates grew faster than revenue over the past several years, a continuing trend of deficits into the future can be expected. Likewise, if the cash ratio is declining, significant cash problems lie ahead.

Trend tables should be put together for the major drivers within revenue, expenses, assets, liabilities, net assets, and cash flow. In addition, tables should track nonfinancial factors such as new students, enrollment, personnel, investment performance, and other factors that drive the financial condition of the institution.

Trend tables should contain roughly three to five years of data, with performance comparisons between the last two years and the total time period covered by the table. Compound rates of growth are used to measure change in non-ratio performance over time periods greater than two years. The resulting compound rate is easier to understand than a simple division of the last year by the first year.[1]

Marginal Analysis

Marginal analysis compares and tracks changes in the dollar values of two financial elements, say tuition revenue and financial aid, from one point in time to another. If tuition revenue increased $250,000 last year but financial aid increased $275,000, then each dollar of new tuition revenue cost $1.10 in financial aid, which would be of obvious concern to an informed president. A well-done marginal analysis will point out how new revenue is being allocated and will make it easy to see if that allocation fits strategic priorities.

Marginal analysis involves computing the actual change in revenue, expenses, assets, liabilities, or net assets to detect how funds or wealth were generated, allocated, expanded, preserved, or diminished. The following table demonstrates one use for marginal analysis.

The table shows what could happen to net tuition if the tuition discount were increased for all students at this hypothetical college: $4.1 million in net tuition would be lost. It's not an unusual scenario: between 1998 and 2001, private colleges raised financial aid 13.9 percent *and net tuition fell 19.4 percent.*[2] Even worse, those colleges saw enrollments slide 16.5 percent despite a substantial increase in tuition discounting.[3]

Multiyear marginal analysis, which requires only a simple rearrangement of data, illuminates dangerous trends. The benefits are certainly worth the effort it takes a chief financial officer to construct a marginal analysis table that captures the revenue, expenses, assets, liabilities, or net assets significant to the institution's financial structure.

Ratio Analysis

Ratio analysis involves the analysis of the relationship of one financial component to another over time. The cash ratio, for example, compares cash to accounts payable to determine whether there is sufficient cash to cover bills due in the near future. Ratios also remove some of the distortion that happens when dollars change over time. Using ratio analysis makes it easier to compare an institution with similar institutions or benchmark groups.

Below is a set of ratios typically used to unearth changes in the most important elements of a financial structure: liquidity, operational performance, debt, and asset management.[4] The section on ratios concludes with a discussion of the composite financial index, which is a mechanism for estimating the financial condition of an institution.

Table 5.1 Marginal Analysis Example

	Yr 1	Yr 2	Yr 3	Yr 1 to Yr 3 Marginal Change
Tuition & Fees	$15,000	$15,250	$15,500	$500
Tuition Revenue	$75,000,000	$79,300,000	$80,677,500	$5,677,500
Financial Aid %	30.0%	35.0%	40.0%	10.0%
Financial Aid	$22,500,000	$27,755,000	$32,271,000	$9,771,000
Net Tuition	$52,500,000	$51,545,000	$48,406,500	–$4,093,500

Liquidity Ratios

Liquidity measures whether there are sufficient current assets, be they cash or sources of cash, to meet short-term cash liabilities. The basic rule is cash is king; without cash the institution is out of business. The liquidity of a noncash assets, such as receivables and inventory, depends on how quickly they can be turned into cash. Some assets converted to cash may not produce their full book value. For example, some portion of student receivables is lost when students cannot—or will not—pay their bills in full. Inventory, in most cases bookstore inventory, also loses much of its value when converted to cash. (A simple way to estimate the conversion loss is to figure what students receive when they trade in a textbook, which is typically lower than 30 percent of the original value, if the book is in good condition.) Liabilities, which unlike liquid assets must be paid in full, affect liquidity when due within a year or less, for example, payables, accruals, and short-term notes payable (credit lines).

Liquid assets and liabilities, also called current assets and current liabilities, respectively, can be measured with the *cash ratio,* which compares cash and short-term investments to current liabilities, short-term obligations that are usually due within a year.

$$Cash\ Ratio = \frac{Cash + Short\ Term\ Investments}{Current\ Liabilities}$$

Operational Performance Ratios

Operational performance measures the relative scale of net income and the major budget factors that influence its production.[5] Of crucial interest to a president is whether negative net income will force the institution to convert endowments to cash and resort to short-term borrowing. Can positive net income sustain an operational expansion of resources? It is imperative that a president understand the dynamics behind net income: the changes in net tuition, gifts, grants, other revenue, compensation, or allocations to other expenses that shape the scale of change in net income.

Revenue and expense ratios should focus on major drivers of net income. When there is a significant change in the value of a ratio, or to the relative balance among ratios, the change should be examined carefully.[6] The issues are whether the reasons for the changes are in line with expectations, or whether the changes are revenue or expenses being driven toward or away from financial goals.

$$Net\ Tuition\ Ratio = \frac{Net\ Tuition}{Total\ Tuition\ and\ Fee\ Revenue}$$

Table 5.2 Liquidity Performance

Ratio	Benchmark	Comment
Cash Ratio	.75 to 1	75 cents of current assets to $1 in current liabilities.

$$\text{Revenue Category Ratio} = \frac{\text{Revenue Category}}{\text{Total Revenue}}$$

$$\text{Expense Category Ratio} = \frac{\text{Expense Category}}{\text{Total Revenue}}$$

An *auxiliary performance ratio* tests the basic rule that auxiliaries should make a positive contribution toward net income, not diminish it. A *net income ratio* obviously indicates if revenues are greater than or less than expenses. Of greater importance, however, is whether net income, if it is positive, is adequate, improving, or turning sour.

$$\text{Auxiliary Performance Ratios} = \frac{\text{Total Expenses for the Auxiliary}}{\text{Total Revenue for the Auxiliary}}$$

$$\text{Net Income Ratio} = \frac{\begin{array}{c}\text{Net Operating Results} \\ \text{from Unrestricted Operations}\end{array}}{\text{Unrestricted Revenue}}$$

Debt

An institution has three principal sources of cash for financing operations and growth: cash flow from operations; net assets; and debt. When acquiring cash from debt, an institution must monitor its capacity to make debt service payments and must know the proportion of its financial resources devoted to debt. A declining capacity to service debt may violate debt covenants. And lenders and credit-rating agencies will disapprove of a glaring debt-to-assets disproportion. (For help in debt-capacity tracking, see the ratios discussed below.)

The *debt service coverage ratio* indicates whether unrestricted resources are sufficient to cover debt. The *viability ratio* measures debt capacity; a ratio below 1.20 suggests questionable capacity.[7] By deducting tangible assets that do not generate income, the *capitalization ratio* denotes the financial flexibility of the institution; a low ratio suggests the institution cannot support more debt, and lenders may indeed be reluctant to loan.[8] Those ratios monitor existing debt and debt capacity only. If the college is subject to ratios stipulated in debt covenants, a board of trustees should certainly include the relevant ratios in all debt considerations.

$$\text{Debt Service Coverage Ratio} = \frac{\begin{array}{c}\text{Change in Unrestricted Net Assets} \\ \text{+ Interest Expense + Depreciation}\end{array}}{\text{Interest Expenses + Principal Payments}}$$

Table 5.3 Operational Performance

Ratio	Benchmark	Comments
Auxiliary Performance Ratio	Greater than 1%	Auxiliaries should yield a positive net.
Net Income Ratio	2% to 4%	Net income should be sustained over several years.

$$Viability\ Ratio = \frac{\overset{\text{Unrestricted + Temporarily Restricted}}{\text{Net Assets}} - \text{Net Fixed Assets} + \text{Long-Term Debt}}{\text{Long-Term Debt}}$$

$$Capitalization\ Ratio = \frac{\text{Net Assets} - \text{Intangible Assets}}{\text{Total Assets} - \text{Intangible Assets}}$$

*Net Fixed Assets = property, plant and equipment net of depreciation

Asset Management Ratios

At most private institutions, survival depends on expanding net assets: deficits drain net assets and restrict a president's ability to respond to unexpected economic threats or changes in the student market. We know that if net income is substantial, net assets increase. Asset management—which utilizes the *return on net assets, return on financial asset investments, physical asset reinvestment,* and *deferred maintenance ratios*—involves assessing whether an institution's investment in fixed and financial assets pays off. Richer endowments might yield larger payouts, but new or aging fixed assets (e.g., buildings, equipment, and land) might place a growing maintenance burden on financial resources.

The *return on net assets ratio* measures change in an institution's wealth by weighing net income against net assets. In some circumstances, a declining ratio is acceptable, for example, a very large ratio will dwindle as a college converts net income to assets or consumes net income in operations. In most circumstances, however, a growing value for the return on net assets is preferred.

The *return on financial asset investments ratio* shows the performance of invested assets. Its benchmark should be a combination of equity, bond, and other market indexes that reflect the composition of an institution's financial assets.[9] If the ratio under-performs its benchmark market index, the investment portfolio and investment policy should be examined.

Table 5.4 Debt

Ratio	Benchmark	Comments
Debt Service Coverage Ratio	2.4 to 4.6	High ratio is preferred, while a low or declining ratio is a cause for concern. Ratio increases with total assets.[a]
Viability Ratio	Greater than 1 to 1	An institution with ratios less than 1 to 1 is in a vulnerable position.[b]
Capitalization Ratio	50% to 85%	The range represents preferred boundaries.[c]

[a]*Source:* Prager, Sealy & Co. Inc., *Strategic Financial Analysis for Higher Education,* 6th ed., 2005, 59–60.

[b]*Source:* Prager, Sealy & Co. Inc., *Strategic Financial Analysis for Higher Education,* 6th ed., 2005, 67–68.

[c]*Source:* Prager, Sealy & Co. Inc., *Strategic Financial Analysis for Higher Education,* 6th ed., 2005, 63–64.

The *physical asset reinvestment ratio* compares reinvestment in physical assets to depreciation. Is the institution maintaining its investment in plant, equipment, and grounds? If capital investment in the plant is not keeping pace with depreciation, that investment may be in jeopardy.

Following from the previous ratio, the *deferred maintenance ratio* compares deferred maintenance to depreciation. If deferred maintenance is too great a proportion of depreciation, the reliability of the plant investment is at risk. Moreover, deferred maintenance could undermine the capacity of an institution to accomplish its mission, to attract students, or to solicit gifts or grants.

$$Return\ on\ Net\ Assets[10] = \frac{Change\ in\ Net\ Assets}{Total\ Net\ Assets\ (beginning\ of\ year)}$$

$$Return\ on\ Financial\ Asset\ Investments[11] = \frac{\begin{array}{c}Investment\ Income + Net\ Realized\ \&\\ Unrealized\ Gains\end{array}}{\begin{array}{c}Average\ Cash\\ + Cash\ Equivalents\ and\ Investments\end{array}}$$

$$Physical\ Asset\ Reinvestment\ Ratio[12] = \frac{Capital\ Expenditures + Capital\ Gifts}{Depreciation\ Expense}$$

$$Deferred\ Maintenance\ Ratio[13] = \frac{Outstanding\ Maintenance\ Requirements}{\begin{array}{c}Unrestricted + Temporarily\ Restricted\ Net\\ Assets- Fixed\ Assets[14] + Long\text{-}Term\ Debt\end{array}}$$

Composite Financial Index

The Composite Financial Index (CFI) was developed by KPMG, and Prager, Sealy & Co. to measure the financial condition of private and public colleges and universities.[15] It is also a tool to identify problems and a mechanism for testing

Table 5.5 Asset Management

Ratio	Benchmark	Comments
Return on Net Assets Ratio	3% to 4% + CPI[a]	Ratio needs to be smoothed over several years. Beware of large investment returns, which distort the ratio.
Return on Financial Asset Investments Ratio	Market Benchmark Indexes	The market benchmark should include market indexes that reflect the composition of the investments; e.g., money market, bonds, and equity indexes.
Physical Assets Reinvestment Ratio	Greater than 1 to 1[b]	Less than 1 to 1 indicates underinvestment in plant.
Deferred Maintenance Ratio	Large ratios are undesirable. Investment and maintenance programs should be evaluated.	

[a]*Source:* Prager, Sealy & Co., Inc., *Strategic Financial Analysis for Higher Education,* 6th ed., 2005, 94.

[b]*Source:* Prager, Sealy & Co., Inc., *Strategic Financial Analysis for Higher Education,* 6th ed., 2005, 81–82.

strategic options. A CFI is calculated by assigning a set of weights and strength factors to an institution's *primary net income, return on net assets, and viability ratios.* Each ratio in a CFI targets a different aspect of a financial structure.

In their experience, the designers of the CFI find the measure to be

> a more balanced view of the state of the institution's finances...possible [using a blended number from the four key ratios] because a weakness in one measure may be offset by the strength of another measure. Second, by using the same criteria to determine the CFI over a period of time, the board and management are given the opportunity to measure the overall financial progress that it is making. Lastly, the measure is easily understood and remembered.[16]

The *primary ratio* is the only ratio in the CFI not covered earlier in this chapter. It suggests how long an institution can continue to operate during periods of extreme financial stress, when deficits are sapping financial resources. The ratio compares net expendable assets (computed by deducting the depreciated value for property, plant, and equipment from unrestricted net assets, temporarily restricted net assets, and long-term debt) to total expenses. Ratio values indicate the proportion of a year during which the institution could operate relying solely on its net expendable assets to support expenses. For example, a .40 value suggests an institution could operate for five months (.40 times 12 months).[17] The following table displays benchmarks and comments about each of the CFI ratios.

The data for the computations come directly from an institution's statements of financial position and activities. A CFO can easily produce scores over several years, with comments on which factors shape changes in the index. The four steps for computing CFI are simple: compute the value for each ratio; convert the ratio values into strength factors (refer to the strength factors in Table 5.7); multiply the strength factors with weighting factors (refer to the weights in Table 5.7); and sum the results to get the CFI score. The strength factors in Table 5.7 are set for a CFI score of 3, which is a threshold value of financial strength.[18] The formula for

Table 5.6 Composite Financial Index Ratios

Ratio	Benchmark	Comment
Primary Ratio	.40[a]	Serious problems are evident for ratios below .10 or .15.
Net Income Ratio	2% to 4%	Net income performance should be sustained over several years.
Return on Net Invested Assets Ratio	Market Benchmark Indexes	Market benchmarks should reflect the composition of the investments.
Viability Ratio	Greater than 1 to 1	An institution with ratios less than 1 to 1 is in a vulnerable position.

[a]*Source:* Prager, Sealy & Co., Inc., *Strategic Financial Analysis for Higher Education,* 6th ed., 2005, 58.

computing a score value for a CFI ratio is [CFI Score Value = *Ratio Value divided by the strength factor times the weight factor* = CFI Score].

The next table shows the ranges for CFI scores with suggestions for action. Scores below 3 that span several years, and especially scores less than zero, should elicit grave concern. Even a one-time low CFI score should inspire a careful assessment of causes and remedial actions.

As the CFI designers noted, the index scores are not precise values, but points in a range that suggest financial condition. Senior management officers will need to interpret the CFI score using their particular knowledge of the institution and of

Table 5.7 Strength Factors at Scale = 3 and Weights for CFI Scoring[a]

Ratio	Strength Factor at Scale	Weight With Long-term Debt	Weight Without Long-term Debt
Primary Reserve Ratio	.4	35%	55%
Net Income Operations Model Ratio	2%	10%	15%
Net Income Change in Unrestricted Net Model Ratio	4.0%	10%	15%
Return on Net Assets Ratio	6.0%	20%	30%
Viability Ratio	1.25	36%	—

[a]*Source:* Prager, Sealy & Co. Inc., *Strategic Financial Analysis for Higher Education,* 6th ed., 2005, 96.

Table 5.8 CFI Scores, Ranges, and Action Statements[a]

CFI Score	CFI Scoring Range	Action
1	−1 to 1	Assess viability of institution's survival.
2	0 to 2	Reengineer the institution.
3	1 to 3	
4	2 to 4	Direct resources toward transformation.
5	3 to 5	
6	4 to 6	Focus resources to compete.
7	5 to 7	
8	6 to 8	Experiment with new initiatives.
9	7 to 9	
10	Greater than 9	Deploy resources to achieve a robust mission.

[a]*Source:* Susan Fitzgerald, "Moody's Rating Approach for Private Colleges and Universities" (New York: Moody's Investors Service, 1999), 1.

the external and internal conditions that affect it. The CFI score must be evaluated *in reference to the component ratios,* which hold the clues to the value of the s core: deconstructing the ratios is a point of departure for designing a financial strategy.

CASE STUDY: SECTION TWO

What Now?

The new president of Rubicon had to act quickly: the college no longer had the cash reserves to support the debt service on its new buildings. He had to determine how to jump-start a turnaround; the college's financial condition; the financial and operational levers to a turnaround; and a turnaround strategic plan with performance controls.

First Steps

The president took hold of the campus by doing the following: rebuilding the board; insisting that all board members contribute; using alumni/ae to recruit students; hiring highly qualified staff; sharing the true financial condition with key faculty; and insisting that faculty and staff stop talking about the demise of the college. The biggest first step was soliciting gifts to cover debt service payments and operating cash flow for two years. Doing that gave Rubicon breathing room while the turnaround strategy was designed and put into operation.

These steps were necessary to build momentum for a turnaround but not sufficient to accomplish the turnaround. The essential component for a turnaround strategy was a deep diagnosis of the college's financial condition.

Financial Condition

In tandem with the preceding steps, the president assigned a task force to *diagnose* the financial condition of the college. The first piece of business was to use the CFI to estimate Rubicon's financial health. CFI tests revealed that between 1993 and 1998, the CFI score hovered between 2.95 and 3.85—okay but not spectacular. Between 2000 and 2003, CFI scores began a descent that resulted in a collapse in 2003: a negative CFI of 1.6. The score only reiterated the obvious. Rubicon was in dire and dangerous straits, on the brink of financial breakdown.

The second question to be analyzed was what made the college tick. Diagnosis began with basic operational and capital data: budget reports, audited statements, enrollment records, personnel changes, cash flow, asset management, debt, and whatever else might tell the story of Rubicon.

Operational data identified *financial drivers,* which are major nodes in the operating system that govern the flow of funds, determine scale, and set the direction of the financial system. Rubicon's income drivers were new students, continuing students, tuition discounts, and auxiliaries. Key expense drivers were administrative and staff compensation, class size, and plant. Cash flow and debt service were also main drivers of the college's financial condition. The president used marginal analysis tables to see how those drivers had pushed the college into severe financial straits. It turned out that financial aid was driving down net tuition, rather than increasing it.

Although tuition and fee revenue shrank 14 percent, net tuition and fees slid from 65 percent to 41 percent of total tuition and fee revenue. Tuition discounts in excess of 60 percent were used to attract new students. Even as net

Figure 5.1 Net to Revenue: Rubicon College

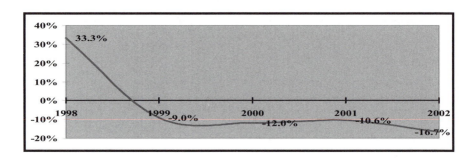

tuition declined, new administrative positions were added; auxiliaries generated deficits; the physical plant absorbed huge amounts of money; cash practically disappeared; working capital was being borrowed at 10 percent above prime; and short and long-term debt grew by leaps and bounds.

Financially, the college was a hollow shell. The deadly strategy of using tuition discounts to support enrollment flowed to the financial system yielding a 24 percent reduction in total net assets. Moreover, its meager investment funds lost 50 percent of their value because they were used to cover cash flow demands.

FINANCIAL TURNAROUND STRATEGY

Many presidents of private institutions back-burner financial strategy because other crises, and daily grinds, usurp valuable time. Presidents must often run marketing efforts; concern themselves with sports teams, class schedules, or cafeteria issues; or respond to midnight dorm emergencies. Though important, such worries take presidents away from larger, strategic issues—both glaring and hidden.

Unbalanced budgets, cash shortfalls, complaints about late payments on debt, and myriad other troubling financial matters will eventually propel financial strategy to the top of the crisis list, and presidents will be highly motivated to make immediate decisions. But systematic consideration of key issues will provide a president the financial strategy necessary to take a college through unexpected market changes.

Strategic Conditions

Four fundamental conditions underlie a successful financial turnaround. First, a financial strategy cannot stand on its own. If it is to be more than another file-bound document, it must fit with academic, marketing, and other strategic plans of the institution. Second, financial transactions must be governed by business policies and procedures and must be heeded and enforced by faculty, staff, and senior leadership. Nothing will devastate a financial strategy or its accompanying budgets faster than willy-nilly purchases, unnecessary job creations, or disregard of the budget. Third, the existing electronic accounting system must produce reliable and timely reports on the financial state of the college, or be replaced. If the system does not capture every transaction in the college, strategic plans will be based on misinformation. Fourth, the leadership must carefully examine its financial condition, lest it base financial strategy on guesswork and wish lists.

Strategic Planning Stages

The successful turnaround strategy will emanate from an enthusiastic president who, with time, money, board support, and community support, will guide the institution through the following methodical stages collection of data; identification of major financial strengths and weaknesses; development of key strategic elements; and establishment of a monitoring system to track variances and respond to internal and external factors that will influence strategic revision.[19]

Data collection starts by setting up trend and marginal analysis tables and selecting appropriate ratios to measure financial performance. Under a president's direction, the chief financial officer with other key managers should select appropriate diagnostic tools and collect data. During that process, leaders must quickly resolve any conflicts or inconsistencies, as financial strategy cannot progress amid unsound data.

Diagnosis starts with a check of the CFI score to see if it is less than three. If so, then the institution needs to use those ratios, in addition to the basic financial ratios described earlier, and along with trend and marginal analysis, to diagnose the underlying financial problems.

The CFI ratios are the fundamental element to identify factors contributing to low scores, because the CFI model will be used as a test bed to evaluate strategic options. Basic financial ratios are evaluated to find other factors that lie outside the purview of the CFI model and that are contributing to the financial weakness of the institution. Debt covenant ratios need to be scrutinized, because ratio values falling outside covenant conditions may lead to the imposition of severe restrictions on financial and operational activity by bondholders, or even calls for immediate repayment of the debt.

While ratios provide significant insight into performance, trend analysis will show where growth rates for factors driving revenue, expenses, assets, liabilities,

Table 5.9 Designing a Turnaround Financial Strategy

Step One:	Design a financial model as a test bed for turnaround strategies.
Step Two:	Identify weak points, using CFI ratios as a primary focus.
Step Three:	Set a target CFI score to be reached by turnaround strategies.
Step Four:	Run the strategies through the financial model.
Step Five:	Prepare full action plans for the accepted turnaround strategies.

net assets, and cash flow are unbalanced. For instance, is short-term net tuition growth lagging long-term growth rates? If those rates are unbalanced, then the relative growth rates for enrollment, tuition, and tuition discounts should be checked to see if tuition discounting is simply cutting into revenue. Trend analysis should continue through all factors driving revenue, expense, asset, liability, or cash trends to reveal other problems lurking within the financial system.

Marginal analysis is another very useful tool because it shows how new monies are allocated and because allocation decisions often follow from incremental decisions that unwittingly shape an institution's financial condition. A marginal analysis of the net tuition example noted above could show that even though more dollars were allocated to tuition discounts, they did not result in increases in net tuition. Marginal analysis may also find that new money is being absorbed by new positions that do not support the main mission of the institution.

The diagnostic report should lay out with considerable precision those factors representing institutional strengths that need to be enhanced as well as weaknesses that must be addressed.

After diagnosis, strategic options should be designed to reduce or eliminate problematic factors identified during the diagnostic stage. The test bed for evaluating strategic options is a comprehensive financial model using variables such as enrollment, tuition, tuition discounts, faculty, staffing, benefits, plant operations, auxiliary services, as well as capital expenditures that drive revenue, expenses, assets, liabilities, net assets, and cash flows. The model should produce at least a five-year forecast, because data based on fewer years might not reveal detrimental trends, and data projected farther out might fail the test of time; for example, student market contingencies cannot be anticipated too far in advance.

Test results from each forecast year should filter into statements of activities, financial position, and cash flow with the results screened using the CFI scoring model with a minimum scoring bar set at three and value limits for ratios established by debt covenant ratios. If the CFI and debt covenant screens prove satisfactory, results should feed into a marginal analysis table to highlight unexpected imbalances that might cause funds to flow in directions counterproductive to the strategic priorities of the institution.

Strategic options that achieve the CFI scoring goal and have met other minimum objectives should be submitted to the president and key leaders for their approval or for their suggestions for alternative strategies (which will require further testing).

There is one final two-part test: for reasonableness. The first is whether the strategies make sense: if enrollment has to increase 80 percent, is it reasonable to assume that that increase can occur within one year? Is it reasonable to assume that sufficient funds can be generated from operations to restore and renovate buildings and equipment? The second is whether the institution has the personnel, policies, and procedures necessary to put the plans into operation. Senior management and the board of trustees should consider both those questions.

After strategic options have been tested, found reasonable, and approved by the president and senior management, a detailed plan should be prepared for their implementation, and the full package should be presented to the board of trustees for review and approval. The entire process—data collection, diagnosis, development of strategic options, testing, and preparation of detailed plans—will be time-consuming and expensive. A tireless and charismatically involved president will be the backbone of a team of board members, faculty, community supporters, and contracted professionals who will contribute energy, knowledge, and fund-raising efforts to the financial turnaround.

CASE STUDY: SECTION THREE

Strategic Levers

The main tool used to test strategic options at Rubicon was the Composite Financial Index; CFI ratios could be directly linked to the critical financial drivers and would provide a reading on the impact that strategic options would have on long-term financial condition of the institution.

The benchmark goal was *a CFI score of 4 or better,* which would move the college beyond the immediate pale of financial failure and allow it to build resources to strengthen its mission. Strategic options were tested by running the data through a five-year financial forecast that modeled financial statements, critical debt covenant ratios, and concluded by computing a CFI score for each year. An option was selected if it met three criteria: it produced a CFI score of 4.0 by year three; it was reasonable; it produced a sustainable income base.

Strategic Plan

The task force found that the following financial options achieved the criteria. (The options did not include a major capital campaign because it had not yet yielded results.)

- Adding four new programs to grow enrollment 7 percent annually
- Keeping tuition increases to 1.5 percent above inflation
- Reducing financial aid by 15 percent
- Expanding class size by 10 percent, which trimmed the number of part-time faculty hired
- Eliminating three academic programs because variable costs were greater than their net revenue
- Cutting 10 administrative and 8 staff positions
- Outsourcing the bookstore, as well as custodial, security, maintenance, and information technology services
- Ending new cars for the key administrators
- Increasing marketing and admission budgets by 40 percent
- Reengineering the work flow for new students, academic counseling, the registrar, and student payments, saving 12 percent of those costs
- Renegotiating bond maturities and payments saving 15 percent of annual debt service expenses
- Leasing 40 acres of unused land for an office park that annually added 5 percent to total revenue

Financial results at the end of fiscal year 2005 indicate that the plan is well on its way to taking hold because the CFI score rose from -1.25 in 2003 to 3.27 in 2005. Admission rates and forecasts for the campaign suggest that the CFI score should come in a range between 3.9 and 4.1 by the end of the 2006 fiscal year. Forecasts for fiscal years 2007 and 2008 indicate that the plan should easily meet its goal of raising the CFI score to 4.0.

Strategic Complements

Evidence from the literature suggests at least 10 keys (see Table 5.10) that are either a foundation for or complement to a successful financial turnaround strategy. Those keys include policies, financial goals based on good business practices, and common sense steps that ensure financial strategies are not undermined by short-sighted actions.

MONITORING TURNAROUND STRATEGIES

No turnaround strategy will succeed unless the president remains fully involved and manifests the discipline necessary to attain strategic goals. Like a parent who leaves the cookie jar open, the president who walks away from a newly established strategy may find greedy, self-interested behavior on the part of others. Monitoring systems that track practices and performance can help to identify if, when, where, and how a financial strategy has been violated.

Table 5.10 Ten Keys to Successful Turnarounds[a]

1.	Balance revenue and expense growth rates.
2.	Estimate revenue conservatively before budgeting expenses, and contain or cut expense growth.
3.	Design a coherent net pricing strategy.
4.	Put into place a consistent foundation for revenue growth.
5.	Build a capital reinvestment fund for renovations and equipment replacement.
6.	Provide a contingency fund and a cash reserve greater than 16 percent of expenses.
7.	Install budget controls to manage over-expended budgets, track variances, and contain the addition of new employees after the start of a new fiscal year.
8.	Bill students monthly and establish collection procedures.
9.	Ensure that college development and alumni relations produce income equal to or greater than their expenses.
10.	Make certain that auxiliary and athletic programs pay their own ways.

[a]*Source:* Michael Townsley, *The Small College Guide to Financial Health* (Washington, DC: National Association of Colleges and Business Officials, 2002), 178–79.

Monitoring should take two forms: tracking strategic performance during the year, and analyzing strategic performance annually, both of which should focus on factors critical to achieving turnaround goals. Reports should be designed to fit the needs of an individual institution, based upon input from the president, chief finance officer, and finance or audit committees of the board.

The *monthly fiscal operations (dashboard) report* is commonly understood to contain budget summaries; cash position; student collections; gifts; grants; capital projects; and critical factors such as enrollment, adjunct positions, new hires, utilities, and other variable factors that drive operational performance. The report should include the main financial drivers so that off-track performance can be caught early, and data must be accurate, timely, and easily understood by readers unskilled in financial analysis. The academic period dashboard should go beyond the narrow scope of the monthly report, which may fail to indicate significant intra-fiscal trends because such changes only become apparent during a longer period, such as an academic semester. The basic elements of those reports should be sufficiently robust for the president and board to see clearly (perhaps with the aid of clarifying statements) what drives the financial condition of the college and whether or not it is holding course.

The *annual financial report*, the multifaceted scorecard that pulls from marketing, academics, student services, and other major activities to reveal whether the college is on track, is critical for an institution going through a financial turnaround. The analysis should compare strategic performance against benchmarks (national, regional, peer, or competition). Key leaders will have to select the performance measures to benchmark. Most institutions use measures that have a direct impact on financial performance found in student flows (e.g., new students, attrition, and graduation) and fund flows (e.g., net tuition, net income, cash, investments, debt, and net assets). If a college begins to lag behind the benchmarks, its competitive position is weakening.

If the annual look at information vital to a college's financial condition reveals a failure in strategy, the report must explain how and why, and suggest when and where management will target efforts to move forward. Time is of the essence in reinvigorating a stalled plan. Delay at the drawing board could thrust the college back into financial crisis.

CASE STUDY: SECTION FOUR

Strategic Performance Controls

Rubicon's strategic plan included operational controls to track strategic goal performance. The controls had two purposes: establish that performance is in line with goals; and determine where plan modifications should take place to achieve those goals.

The college developed two reporting formats beyond the usual financial and operational reports to track strategic performance: student flow and financial flow reports. The student flow report tracks students from inquiry through admissions, matriculation, attrition, and graduation. The financial flow report tracks income as it enters through major revenue sources, through expenses, and then to net income, cash, investments, debt, and net assets. The president has established the strategic guideline that the college will reevaluate its plans if there is a significant decline in trends, or if the college begins to lag behind its benchmark competitors.

COMMENTS ON FINANCIAL STRATEGIES

Leadership

A president must initiate comprehensive, campus-wide strategic planning to anchor the financial strategy. Admissions must bring in more students; academic departments must offer new programs or invigorate stale ones; legitimate gifts must be found; and new tough goals, with time limits and oversights, must be established. The president and senior management must set, and maintain, both a rigorous pace and tough standards for all involved.

Money

Too often, financial turnarounds at threadbare institutions are based upon the luck of the draw. A new president with no relevant experiences—often the only type who will take on a difficult turnaround—had better be a marketing genius. Money for planning, prettying up the campus, and keeping the doors open for the year that it will take to hammer out a financial turnaround strategy must be scraped from every possible source. And the expenses will be considerable: using consultants to develop a turnaround plan can cost between $50,000 and $250,000. New programs, marketing plans, or building renovations will add several hundred thousand more. Though a huge sum, a nickel-and-dime approach might just get an institution through the current crisis and on to the next, at least until a strategy can be put into place.

Revised Work Flows

If an institution is in financial crisis, current interoffice work and student processing flows aren't acceptable. Despite the near palpable wish of employees that everything stays the same until the crisis blows over, a president must shift and terminate jobs based upon who has pulled his or her weight so far and who will pull it harder over the coming months. While preparing devoted employees for streamlined operations, rigidly designed paper trails, and overhauled administrative systems, the president must also prepare to welcome as many new and happy students as possible. Increasing admission and retention rates will require sprucing up dorms and improving food services, classrooms, and bookstore operations as well.

Revised Policies and Procedures

Policies and procedures must lend themselves to student success. Too often administrative requirements exist for the convenience of the administration, rather than that of students. Most students, particularly adult students, have little patience with policies or procedures that get between them and their long-sought degrees. Likewise, policies and procedures that guide everyday business practices should be simple and direct. If purchase approval is required, it must be secured, or else consequences must follow. Partially followed business practices can bump a weak institution over the edge to failure.

CONCLUSION

Leadership, support, money, discipline, planning, and smart implementation, the critical components of a successful financial strategy, go way beyond ratios and CFI scores. We already know a president must be a miracle worker, beggar, psychologist, marketing wizard, and babysitter. Budget cuts will be made, employees disgruntled, senior ranks depleted, and student feathers ruffled in order to make the changes most fundamental to an institution's long-term survival. Smooth change is an unrealistic expectation, so leaders must expect resistance and complaint, long hours and sleeplessness, before new ideas can take hold and messages of hope can self-prophesize. Presidents can make their job easier with a board that understands and supports their actions. With effort and assistance, and before the eyes of the unbelievers sharing the gurney with a president determined to pull an institution back from the verge of financial death, miracles can happen.

CASE STUDY CONCLUDED: SECTION FIVE

Where is Rubicon Now?

Performance reports show that the college has begun the turnaround. Although two years do not make for a long-term turnaround, they do set the stage for the future. The strategic plan is shrinking the gap with its competitors because they are well positioned with net tuition, and cash reserves are approaching their benchmark goals.

Rubicon has had to tweak its plan. Changes have been made to enrollment goals for specific academic program, marketing expenses, cash reserves, and plant goals.

The president believes that Rubicon can survive for the long term only if it goes through a paradigm shift, which should encompass the cost of delivering education and the type of education that is delivered. Strategic planning for that massive change is expected to begin during the summer of 2007, which will be the fourth year of the turnaround.

But there are signs that the board is reviving its old feud between athletic boosters and businesspeople. Some members want the school to find a glorious future by moving from Division III to Division I in the NCAA and want to institute a massive capital campaign for financial aid, a huge new stadium, and an all-sports coliseum. While the president was able to deflect their outlandish dreams for the moment, it is apparent that the old jocks will eventually prevail. Without much ado, the president has begun to extend feelers for a new challenge. Thus the ultimate success of the financial turnaround is questionable.

NOTES

1. The formula for figuring a compound rate of change is $\{FV/PV \wedge (1/t)\}$ where FV = future value or value for the last year; PV = the present value or value for the first year; $\wedge$ = raising the first term (FV/PV) by the second term $(1/t)$; t = the number of periods.

2. Michael T. Townsley, "Recognizing the Unrealized," *Business Officer,* March 2005, 32.

3. Ibid.

4. Find more about those tools in Prager, Sealy & Co., LLC; KPMG LLP; and Bearing Point, Inc., *Strategic Financial Analysis for Higher Education,* 6th ed. (Washington, DC: National Association of College and University Business Officers, 2005).

5. Accounting rules treat net income as a change in the value of net assets reported in the *statement of financial position.*

6. These revenue and expense ratios are revisions of the ratios found in Prager, Sealy & Co., *op. cit.* The revisions bring the ratios into a standard format to identify either the contribution to total revenue or the demand on total revenue by major expense categories.

7. Ibid., 87.

8. Ronald E. Salluzzo, Philip Tahey, Frederic J. Prager, and Christopher J. Cowen, *Ratio Analysis in Higher Education,* 4th ed. (New York: KPMG and Prager, McCarthy & Sealy, LLC, 1999), 21–22.

9. Prager, Sealy & Co. Inc., 60.

10. Salluzzo et al., *op. cit.,* 62–63.

11. Prager, Sealy & Co. Inc., *op. cit.,* 73–74.

12. Salluzzo et al., *op. cit.,* 62–63. (The ratio has been modified to include only financial assets; physical assets were excluded.)

13. Prager, Sealy & Co. Inc., *op. cit.,* 77–78.

14. Net Fixed Assets = property, plant, and equipment net of depreciation.

15. Prager, Sealy & Co. Inc., *op. cit.,* 77–78.

16. Michael T. Townsley, Financial Planning Toolbox (Washington, DC: National Association of Colleges and Business Officials, 2004), 81.

17. Prager, Sealy & Co. Inc., *op. cit.,* 94.

18. Townsley, *Financial Planning,* 87.

19. Susan Fitzgerald, "Moody's Rating Approach for Private Colleges and Universities" (New York: Moody's Investors Service, 1999), 1.

CHAPTER 6

Turnarounds in Public Higher Education

Terrence MacTaggart

"Be Bold!" an enthusiastic member of the chattering class exhorted a new public college president during the heyday of the reinventing government movement of the 1990s. Apostles of public sector reform like David Osborne, political leaders, and an army of followers set about reengineering the public sector to be more lean, efficient, and customer oriented.[1] Many in higher education, carried along by the euphoria of the times, felt that a new era of change was about to dawn in their conservative bailiwicks whose roots lay in the Middle Ages.

To be sure, some important and lasting attitude shifts have occurred since those heady times. There is now a greater awareness of the student as customer, there are better efforts to quantify the value added by college, and there is a greater sensitivity to results than there once was. But one does not have to be excessively morose to agree with Robert Birnbaum that many of the ideas inspired by the reinventing government movements amounted to fads that have come and gone without much lasting change.[2]

In fact, "be realistic, politically attuned, and patient" would have been more helpful advice. Compared to those of the private sector, turnarounds, and other significant changes in public higher education, come about less fully, more slowly, and only after dealing with trenchant political and bureaucratic barriers. But they *do* occur, when skilled leaders overcome the forces that inhibit change, and especially when those leaders are able to successfully tap public monies to support such turnarounds.

Trustees familiar with getting things done in the relatively unfettered world of the modern corporation need to learn the realities of the public sector early in their tenures. Accentuating the gap between the two sectors, the president of a large public utility company (not the least regulated industrial sector, to be sure) bluntly told a public university counterpart, "I can lay off 500 people if I have to. You can't."

Accustomed to clear understandings within their organizations of the lines of authority, and in agreement that getting decisions made and carried out in a timely way is a good thing, trustees fresh from the corporate boardroom encounter an unfamiliar world when they enter public higher education. They frequently find the change very frustrating.

Thus new trustees from the corporate world will find this chapter especially enlightening—or perhaps troubling—because it argues that the change strategies suited to the for-profit sector are unlikely to work in public higher education. Naturally enough, the lessons of leadership in the for-profit world are the lessons those trustees know best. And indeed, the expectations for higher standards of fiscal stewardship and integrity, required for corporations by the Sarbanes-Oxley legislation, spill over to the benefit of public sector trusteeship. Still, actually exercising demanding standards of oversight often proves daunting to trustees inexperienced in the pace of public sector change.

After discussing the distinctive features of public sector turnarounds that set them apart from private sector transformations, this chapter presents two illustrative cases. The first is a failed attempt to restructure a public system of higher education, and the other the successful turnaround story of the University of Connecticut. The first case illustrates how turnaround ideas that have been tested in the corporate sector often fail to work in the nonprofit world. By contrast, UConn is moving from a mediocre safety school in the brand-conscious world of New England higher education to a preeminent research university. The chief lesson of UConn's transformation is that to achieve success in turning around public universities, leaders must alternatively manage and exploit the dynamics of change in the public sector.

COMMON FEATURES OF PUBLIC SECTOR TURNAROUNDS

The turnaround at the College of New Jersey described in chapter 4 and the case of the University of Connecticut, among others, illustrate that savvy educational leaders who can circumvent bureaucratic barriers and link academic goals to what the public wants can implement turnarounds in public colleges and universities. Such turnarounds are distinctly different from those of their private sector counterparts.

Public Sector Turnarounds Take Longer

By the time he retires in September 2007, Philip Austin will have presided over the ongoing turnaround at the University of Connecticut for 11 years, and that transformation began a year before he arrived. Harold Eickhoff was president at the College of New Jersey for 19 years (1980–98) before passing the responsibility for continuing the turnaround there to Bobbi Gitenstein, who has led the college for seven years. Adrian Tinsley, credited with transforming the very ordinary regional Bridgewater State College of Massachusetts into one of the finest institutions of its kind, took 13 years to do the job. And the legendary Charles McClain who turned Northeast Missouri State University into a nationally heralded liberal arts institution, by focusing relentlessly on what students actually know and can do as a result of their education, stayed at the helm for nearly 20 years (1970–89). He also secured a name change for the rebranded school to Truman State University. Those five leaders have each served an average of almost 14 years, more than twice the average term of public college presidents.

Would we see more transformations of mediocre public institutions into higher performing ones if their executives stayed longer? There is no universal answer to that question. Much good can be accomplished in half a decade or less, and a case can be made that after five to seven years there is a marked decline in the effectiveness of many presidents.[3] And sometimes, of course, five years is far too long. But suffice to say that presidential tenure at the public turnaround schools we observed is more like that at independent institutions. Short-term presidencies don't produce positive long-term results.

But there is another reason why it takes so much longer to transform a publicly supported college or university, or a system. The short and correct explanation is because the power to lead change is widely distributed. Faculty senates and assemblies, employee unions, and other influential political groups within universities tend to prefer the status quo to something new. Not only are such groups influential in their own rights, they often have immense sway with legislators who control the purse strings. Added to that political reality is the omnipresence in many states of regulatory bureaucracies controlling finances, capital construction, human resources, and other operational features. The result is that presidents and trustees are literally caught in the middle, and left with far less authority than their counterparts at private colleges and universities.[4]

Higher Bottom, Lower Top

Earlier in this book, we described turnarounds as having three stages. Stage I focuses on the restoration of financial health at fiscally distressed schools. State II emphasizes marketing academic programs and branding or repositioning the institution to a more attractive niche in the marketplace. Revitalizing the academic and cultural core of the institution occurs in Stage III. We noted that those stages often overlap and are integrated, and that not all institutions need to pursue them in the fixed order. Thanks to state financial support on the one hand and to the constraints to change on the other, turnarounds at public institutions tend to operate in what we have characterized as Stage II.

Because of their financial safety net, public institutions are less likely to have to pursue the Stage I financial reforms essential at struggling private sector colleges. At the same time, the relatively greater power of faculty and staff, especially if unionized, makes it infinitely more difficult to reallocate resources from lower- to higher-priority needs at public colleges. Those same forces, along with the high-access mission of most public institutions, make it harder to bring about the profound academic change found in Stage III revitalizations. Thus, much of what passes for turnarounds in the public environment occurs in the realm of Stage II.

To be sure, market repositioning at an institution occurs with students, their families, and others who influence their educational choices—high school guidance counselors and employers, for instance. But turnarounds at public institutions need also to restore confidence in the minds of the politicians who fund them.

Public institutions face special difficulties in trying to reposition themselves as –higher-quality places. In return for public funding, the state expects that public institutions will be hospitable to a broad range of students. When quality is defined in terms of selectivity, public institutions face a disadvantage. Although the best public universities have relatively stringent admissions hurdles, they are required to be less selective than their counterparts in the private sector. So even the so-called public ivies such as the University of Michigan and the University of Virginia do not rise to the very top of the rankings that prize selectivity. Indeed, the highest ranking public institution in *U.S. News & World Report's* 2007 "National Universities: Top Schools" category, is the University of California, Berkeley, which appears at number 21. As the transformation at the University of Connecticut suggests, however, public universities can move up the academic chain of being when the climb to a stronger reputation for excellence is linked to broad public purposes.

Access as Fairness

To be sure, bringing solid educational opportunity to large numbers of students is an important civic value. The great liberal social philosopher John Rawls argues that in a capitalist society, it is only fair and just that all citizens be given access to the tools necessary for acquiring material goods. He writes that education should be provided to improve the material well-being of all citizens, including those with the lowest incomes. He goes further to say that all members of society, including the least favored, deserve the intrinsic, personal benefits that education brings. Social justice, according to Rawls, requires that "resources for education are not to be allocated solely or necessarily mainly according to their return as estimated in productive or trained abilities, but also according to their worth in enriching the personal and social life of citizens, including here the less favored."[5]

That concept of access to education as access to greater material well-being, and to the good life, generally underpins public investment in education at all levels. Indeed, the idea of "quality" in higher education could be redefined to include the numbers of people who directly benefit from it such that if we evaluated two schools with equal standards, we would judge the larger one better. But for the most part, America's definition of quality overlaps with prestige and exclusivity, not with generous admissions policies.

Politics as the Key to Survival

If public institutions rarely make the very top tier, seldom do they go bankrupt. The few schools that have shut their doors did so primarily because they lacked political advocates powerful enough to keep them open. In the early 1990s, a branch of the University of Minnesota in the farm country of rural Waseca closed not because of high costs, but because system leaders felt they needed to shed a nondescript unit as part of their strategic commitment to greater excellence. Local advocates could not secure the political support to prevent the closing. Interestingly, at about the same time a similar branch in Crookston, which enjoyed the strategic advantage of a location in the district represented by the president of the state senate, grew from a two-year to a four-year institution. The campus in Waseca became a state prison, which likely cost the state far more than the college had. Furthermore, it is unlikely that the University of Minnesota's reputation for excellence was much altered by either change in its rural campuses.

Lacking the sense of urgency generated by a true fiscal crisis, and constrained by the interest groups and politics of the public sector, turnarounds at public institutions don't linger in Stage I. While reduced funding may lead to some layoffs and spending limits, and individual employees affected by these circumstances experience a personal economic crisis, the survival of the institution itself is never in doubt. Instead, the most common kind of turnaround is a limited one of restoring public confidence and instilling a sense of momentum.

Where the Money Is

If public university presidents feel like Swift's Gulliver, strapped to the ground by many tiny threads woven by myriad small-minded bureaucrats and politicians, their cash-strapped private college counterparts are envious of public financial support. Consider the following example: A comprehensive state school with 10,000–15,000 students might receive a state appropriation of about $100 million each year. Assume that the school received no state support, that it needed to rely on student tuition and fees for 75 percent of its budget, and that the rest, $25 million, came from an endowment that paid out 5 percent of its principle. That hypothetical university would need an endowment of $500 million, which would put it in a league with Brandeis University and Northeastern University. Should the *entire* state contribution have to come from endowment, the amount climbs to about $2 billion—the endowment of fewer than 20 of the top research universities in the country.

If there are plenty of Lilliputian strings attached to the monies public institutions receive, they do receive a good bit. In a 2000 bond referendum, citizens of the state of North Carolina agreed to invest $2.5 billion in new infrastructure and buildings on the system's 16 campuses. As a requirement for those funds, however, the colleges were to raise an additional 40 percent of that amount. And they more than succeeded, bringing in about $2.7 billion. The new look of the campuses is considered one of the reasons why the total system enrollment has grown from about 160,000 students in the 1990s to a projected enrollment of nearly 200,000 in 2007.

The state of Connecticut fueled the turnaround at UConn by making an investment of about $2.3 billion in the physical plant. The result is a spectacularly rebuilt campus. Only the richest private institutions can raise that kind of money. And as the UConn case illustrates, in the public sector it goes only to those institutions and systems with adroit leaders who capitalize on their public sector status.

WHEN CULTURES COLLIDE: A FAILED TRANSFORMATION

General Motors and Ford are at this writing engaged in a desperate battle for survival as corporations. Their turnaround strategies involve massive layoffs, plant closings and consolidations, and givebacks from their unionized employees. They will attempt to bring to market hybrid fuel vehicles, along with other new products to compete with Japanese and Korean automakers, but critical to their success is a thorough operational restructuring to bring their unit costs closer to those of the competition. On a much smaller scale, the case that follows describes an attempt to initiate a turnaround by consolidating campus units within a public higher education system.

The case presented here illustrates how *not* to engineer turnarounds in public sector higher education. It was begun with the best of intentions and designed by intelligent, experienced trustees. It failed because it ignored the realities of bringing change to institutions where trustees must share power broadly and where legislators, not trustees, are really the ultimate authority on higher education policy. The case is not hypothetical, although in keeping with the practice in this book in presenting less than successful cases, the name of the system will remain anonymous.

Faced with stagnant state support, projected sharp enrollment declines, and stubborn resistance from donors to contribute to operational costs, a handful of veteran trustees of a public university system determined that a bold new strategy was necessary. Although their plan later came to embrace a host of more conventional initiatives, the first thrust of their effort was to combine three small campuses into one and to merge a fourth with a larger sister institution within commuting distance. Located at the northern and eastern fringes of the state, the small campuses experienced low enrollments—the largest enrolled about a thousand students—high per-student costs, and modest reputations outside their regions.

Saving money was a major goal of the initiative, although improved academic quality, along with greater access to graduate programs through distance education and shared faculty appointments, were also desired outcomes. According to its proponents, the strategic plan would turn around the fortunes of the smaller, even beleaguered, institutions by making them more efficient and academically attractive. No one addressed the problem of how the loss of traditional campus names in favor of a common, generic one would affect brand recognition and campus identity. And nearly everyone involved downplayed the possibility of negative community reactions to having "their" colleges taken away.

"Dead on Arrival"

In the abstract, the idea of combining smaller, less economical units into larger, more efficient ones made sense. Executives at General Motors would have no trouble understanding the strategy. Basic microeconomic thinking holds that increasing scale reduces unit costs. Even if the educational synergies—combined faculty positions, a shared curriculum—proved elusive, consolidating purely administrative functions—admissions and student financial aid, for example—promised to reduce some costs. At the same time that it proposed the two mergers, the system was installing a new enterprise-wide information system. That technology, it was argued, would support the integration.

Had the system been governed like GM or Ford, the strategy might have worked. Had the university system overseen a network of branches, each with a centrally appointed manager, the scheme could have been implemented, and might have produced the expected savings and efficiencies. Of course, the governance realities in the case were different. Public higher education systems are bureaucracies enmeshed in a political environment. The authority to make strategic decisions is decentralized to powerful campus and regional political and economic interests on the one hand and the governor's office and legislature on the other. Public college trustees ignore those realities at their peril.

In this instance, the legislature summarily rejected the proposed mergers. The debate over whether politicians or lay trustees ruled the system roiled the state but was settled unequivocally in favor of the legislature. The trustees' plan, as one influential legislator put it, was "dead on arrival" at the state house.

What Went Wrong?

With the benefit of hindsight, it appears the planners failed to recognize, or abide by, three fundamental realities of the public sector. First, although certainly aware of sunshine laws, the trustees in this case apparently felt they would not be required to open up the plan to the press until they were ready. Second, they failed to inform any of those who would be most affected by their plans: faculty, staff, community leaders, or legislators. Finally, they seemed to disregard the fundamental realities of governing a state system of higher education.

Secret Plans

Freedom of information statutes require that public agencies and boards conduct most of their business in sessions open to anyone who wishes to attend. The laws, which also give the public, including journalists, access to written documents, extend well beyond those affecting private institutions and corporations. Frequent exceptions to those openness requirements are discussions of personnel or legal matters, real estate transactions, and employee contract negotiations. Unfortunately for the board, however, even though its plan would affect personnel, the planning process itself did not qualify for an exemption to the sunshine laws. Their secrecy would come back to haunt the members of the board of trustees.

In spite of the theoretical logic of the turnaround plan, even its champions admitted in retrospect that the rollout was deeply flawed. Most of the planning involved the trustees alone, without formal input from those who would be most affected. For months, however, rumors spread among the campus presidents, faculty senates, and union assemblies about the plan's components. Eventually, that speculation reached the press. When a local newspaper requested a copy of the plan under the state's freedom of information laws, the trustees had no choice but to comply. Thus, many policymakers, university employees, and community leaders learned the details of the plan over their morning coffee. Officials of the towns whose campuses were to be merged were highly indignant. Their campuses were a source of pride and prestige. They represented an accessible, low-cost source of higher education for local youth. And they also provided well-paying jobs for many local citizens.

Once the plans became public, the trustees had lost their opportunity to engage all the stakeholders. Although they called a series of hasty meetings across the state, they were never able to mount an effective offense; they were forced to defend themselves without time to prepare.

Lack of Faculty Involvement

The trustees also excluded the very faculty, staff, and administrators whose support of the plan would have been essential to its success. Believing, probably correctly, that those internal constituents would have demand compromises in the merger plan had they been part of the process, the trustees consciously operated within a very closed circle. When the plan saw the light of day, responses ranged from skepticism to outrage. In the end, campuses that felt they might benefit from the changes supported the effort. Those who felt themselves disadvantaged, however, were passionate in their opposition.

Earlier in this book, we pointed out that successful Stage I turnarounds, those aimed at restoring financial health, require high levels of transparency, as well as thoughtful engagement of faculty and other staff in the process. In this case, the faculty and staff might have been employees of the system, but they were also constituents of important legislators and engaged members of their communities at large. And their state representatives quickly embraced their visceral, negative reactions to the planned mergers.

Ignoring Political Realities

The third mistep was to forget the golden rule of the public sector—those who have the gold make the rules. Fortunately most legislators don't insist on making *all* the rules for higher education, but they do expect to be consulted and heeded on changes of real magnitude. As mentioned, an influential state senator representing the district that was home to one of the campuses to be merged announced that the plan would be dead on arrival at the statehouse. That expression of realpolitik proved to be the case. Although the drama took some months to play out, and the plan's noncontroversial elements gradually received more attention, in the end all the campus consolidations were scrapped.

Had the announcement been better managed, indeed, had influential stakeholders been part of the planning process itself, the dramatic changes envisioned in the plan would have been better received. But it is doubtful that they would have been enacted in their original form. Mergers of independent colleges or universities are more apt to be successful in part because the entities voluntarily join together. Sometimes labeled "mutual growth" mergers, in such cases the very survival of one or both of the entities is really at stake, and both entities believe they will be better off together than alone.[6]

Mergers in the public sector usually come about only when they are mandated by the legislature and seldom occur without at least legislative acquiescence.[7] Whether they actually work in achieving their original purposes of saving money and producing greater efficiency is another matter.

UCONN: BECOMING "A GREAT STATE UNIVERSITY"

The mission statement of the University of Connecticut, adopted in 1975, makes the university's ambitions clear. It begins, "The mission of the University of Connecticut is to be a great state university. This means providing education of a quality equal to that offered by the best public universities in the nation." The mission goes on to link that aspiration to greatness with public purposes, and with wealth of the state with the nation's highest per-capita income. UConn, the mission continues, "must serve a citizenry which demands and has a right to expect excellence in a state which is highly developed technologically." In 1994, UConn's board of trustees went further: "UConn will be perceived and acknowledged as the outstanding public university in the nation—a world-class university."

To be sure, the statement proceeds for six more pages in paying homage to undergraduate education, access, the land grant mission, accountability, and so forth. But the unqualified commitment to becoming first-rate sets Connecticut's mission apart. It is also almost unique in that UConn is well on the way to actually making good on the claim. Since President Phil Austin arrived in the fall of 1996, UConn has followed a nearly smooth upward trajectory, fueled by massive state investment in physical facilities.

Like the precision shooting of its five-time women's basketball NCAA champions, in its climb to the top UConn's leadership team has done almost everything right. And when it stumbles, as occurred when fire code violations in three of the 53 new buildings under construction became highly publicized, the team recovers quickly, and demonstrates appropriate humility for mistakes, along with a determination not to repeat them.

"A Neglected Embarrassment"

The story of UConn's turnaround begins with a handful of university employees, advised by some former legislative operatives. The talented and politically savvy group came to believe in 1994 that the time was right for major state investment in the deteriorated university. Recognizing that in political alchemy, bad news can be turned into gold, they resolved that a dramatic makeover of the dilapidated campus would be the centerpiece of their proposal. They found strong encouragement from Thomas D. Ritter, the speaker of Connecticut's House of Representatives, who is now a trustee of UConn.

The campus at Storrs was widely regarded, in the words of the *Hartford Courant*, the state's leading newspaper, as a "neglected embarrassment" and a "laughing stock." As the newspaper pointed out, it was "the shoddily built Homer Babbidge Library, sheathed in plastic for years, that gave rise to the unprecedented capital investment."[8] Thus UConn 2000, a $1 billion investment in the transformation of a campus from a source of ridicule to a national showpiece, was born.

With Ritter's active support, and with the approval of a bipartisan group of legislators, UConn 2000 was developed in 1994 and funded by the legislature in the following session. None of that was accidental, of course. An ably led grassroots communications and advocacy effort stressed the theme that the state deserved a first-rate university and a campus transformation was the way to achieve greatness. While the success of the women's basketball team, or the men's team's two national championships as well, could not have been planned, university leaders took full advantage of the state's identification with the success of its sports heroes. Shortly before a key legislative vote authorizing the funds for UConn 2000, for example, members of the victorious women's team visited legislators in the statehouse to help make the case.

New Curb Appeal

A second surge of funding effort, 21st Century UConn, begun in 2002, has brought the total capital investment from $2.3 billion to $2.8 billion. At this writing, the university is about halfway through the process of using those resources to remake the campus. The project has been described as "the most ambitious publicly funded building program for any single public university in the nation."[9] More than 30 new academic and residential buildings, including facilities for chemistry, business, computing, biology, physics, biotechnology, and pharmacy, are either completed or under way.

But more important to the UConn turnaround than the additional square footage and the shiny new equipment is the total effect of what amounts to a new campus at the old location. One observer refers to its "curb appeal" in reinvigorating the spirit of the university and making it a desired destination for talented students. "Very hot" is how guidance counselors describe the appeal of the Storrs campus to high school graduates and their parents. Whether or not they are familiar with the old Storrs campus, visitors marvel at the uniform attractiveness of the new one.

The transformation from safety school to university of choice between 1995 and 2005 is impressive. During that period, applications have nearly doubled (to more than 19,000 from 9,874) for the approximately 3,200 slots in the first-year class. The numbers of enrolling valedictorians and salutatorians went from 40 to more than 100, while the mean SAT scores rose by 76 points. Minority enrollments at both Storrs and the regional campuses have more than doubled, with the larger increases occurring at the main campus itself. Finally, once they enroll at UConn, students appreciate the experience and remain through graduation. Currently the conversion from first- to second-year students is more than 90 percent—a remarkable achievement at a public institution, and very respectable when compared to the best private research universities as well.

The attractiveness of UConn to graduating high school students has helped the state of Connecticut address its brain drain of talented students to other states. Prior to UConn 2000, Connecticut exported, on a per-capita basis, more of its brightest than any other state save Alaska. That trend has been reversed: 58 percent of its high school seniors who go to college prefer to remain in state, with many of them enrolling at Storrs or one of UConn's regional campuses.

Although UConn came late to private fund-raising, it is catching up fast. In the summer of 2004, the university formally closed its capital campaign at $471 million, well above the original $300 million target. Since 1995, the endowment has climbed nearly sevenfold, from $42 million to about $270 million, and annual giving approaches $60 million. The university's single largest donors, Ray and Carole Neag, have given $10 million to support cancer research and another $21 million to the School of Education. The latter is the single largest gift ever made to a public university in New England.

UCONN AS PARABLE

UConn's rapid turnaround and stellar trajectory are certainly exceptional in the world of public higher education. State support for operating expenses has dropped in Connecticut from about half of the campus budget to about 36 percent, which matches a national trend. But the sheer magnitude of the state's capital investment, and the audacity of President Phil Austin and his team in putting the money to use quickly and effectively, set UConn apart. And the principles involved in UConn's dramatic turnaround apply to transformations everywhere, and especially those in the public sector.

The turnaround at the University of Connecticut offers important lessons for trustees and other leaders. Some of these lessons apply to any turnaround at any type of university. Others are unique to the public sector.

A High-Performing Board

In addition to a clear mission, an able team of administrative leaders, and strong state support, UConn has been gifted with a very good board of trustees. Twelve of the members are appointed by the governor and confirmed by the state legislature. The other nine members comprise elected student and alumni representatives, and there are five ex officio members, including the governor. That selection process has worked well for UConn, in that the trustees are broadly representative of institutional and state interests, dedicated to advancing the university, and ably led. There is healthy give-and-take among trustees, a willingness to periodically evaluate their own performance as a board, as well as solid support for the transformation.

The quality of the board became apparent during the turmoil that surrounded the university's discovery of fire code violations in three of its 53 new named buildings. The issue became a cause célèbre in the press and was exacerbated by individuals who felt that UConn had attracted a bit too much public support. The governor appointed a special commission to review the status of construction oversight, and the university's capacity to manage the remake of the campus became a matter of public debate. The commission eventually confirmed that UConn, and not the state bureaucracy that oversaw construction in the past (and was responsible for the shabby facilities that had plagued UConn), should remain in charge of the reconstruction program.

This vote of confidence in the university came about in part because Phil Austin was quick to accept responsibility, and, led by its very able chair, John Rowe, M.D., the board was equally quick to take action to correct the mistakes. The trustees moved decisively as well to strengthen their own internal audit function and to seek independent verification from an external audit firm. The chair and other influential trustees, including Tom Ritter, met with political leaders and opinion makers to reassure them that UConn 2000 was being well managed.

Progress by the Numbers

Connecticut is noteworthy in its systematic use of peer comparisons to track its upward progress. In its annual report on its progress to the board of trustees, UConn measures itself against a group of schools that might be described as aspirational peers, and looks back at a previous peer group, which it feels it has surpassed. In 2004, the aspirational peers included Ohio State University, Purdue University, the University of Georgia, and the main campus of the University of Minnesota. The second group included Colorado State University, the University of West Virginia, and, interestingly, UConn's neighbor to the north, the University of Massachusetts at Amherst.

The board is informed on UConn's performance compared to both those groups on several educational, social, and reputational variables. For example, at any given time trustees and the campus as a whole can compare the university's performance to others' in terms of graduation rates, student-faculty ratios, minority representation, research awards, alumni giving, and rankings in *U.S. News & World Report*. That relentless attention to comparative metrics underpins UConn's determination to move upward in the ranks of public research universities.

A Public Agenda

UConn's transformation has been colored by its position as the preeminent public institution in the state. As the land grant university, UConn has a responsibility not only to seek educational excellence for the sake of the university and the faculty but to support a *public* agenda that directly or indirectly serves the people of the state as well.

Prior to the turnaround at its largest public institution, the large number of students who left the state was a public embarrassment. It was also seen as a serious detriment to the long-term future of Connecticut's high-tech economy. And, in a state with such high individual and family incomes, many found it galling that a large number of high school students simply did not go to college.

Coinciding with the rise of UConn as a hot school, much of that has changed. Connecticut is still a net exporter of students to neighboring states, but the numbers have been cut nearly in half. Connecticut's net loss was about 4,600 in that educational balance of trade in 1992. By 2004, the loss had been reduced to 2,352.

While it is hard to draw absolutely a causal link between the decline in the brain drain and the rise of UConn as a name brand, there is logic in connecting the two. Connecticut's college-going young people had long been lured to the myriad excellent colleges in neighboring states. Institutions in New York, Rhode Island, and Massachusetts have not lost their luster, but UConn has gained some. As a consequence, it seems reasonable to conclude that more Connecticut students are deciding to attend their home institution. One can only expect that keeping those talented students in state, and attracting more competitive students from other states as well, bodes well for the economic and social future of Connecticut.

Orchestrating Political Support

Without the massive state investment, UConn's transformation would have taken much longer to unfold, had it occurred at all. Insiders who helped engineer public support for UConn 2000 often use the word "magic" to describe how the political stars aligned to bring about the initial billion-dollar investment. But there was plenty of skill as well, demonstrated by those who orchestrated a well-designed grassroots campaign in support of the investment and by others who worked the statehouse as artfully as any corporate lobbyist.

In the private sector, immense energy and technical skill are devoted to analyzing the donor base and cultivating donors to contribute to campaigns, buildings, and endowment. Many public sector institutions are now pursuing those same individuals and philanthropic organizations. But the most important donor for public institutions remains the state. And a high level of skill, as well as systematic effort, is required to maintain effective relations with that, sometimes prickly, friend of the university.

Deregulation

In the early 1990s, the university gained substantial independence from the state agency that had theretofore supervised all public construction projects, including those at universities. During the same period, the legislature reduced the authority of the state's coordinating board for higher education. In doing so, Connecticut followed a nationwide pattern that included New Jersey, where the state coordinating board was eliminated, and local campus boards were named to take its place.[10] Maryland also reduced the authority of its statewide boards and enabled two public institutions—St. Mary's College and Morgan State University—to establish their own independent boards.[11]

It is difficult to overestimate the importance of the devolution of authority for university management from a state agency to the UConn board. One observer close to the scene argues that the turnaround simply could not have occurred under the "one size fits all" rule-making mentality of state bureaucracies. Another asserted that the new independence was nearly as important as the state billions in underpinning UConn's transformation.

THE CONTRASTS

Leaders of the University of Connecticut did almost everything right in their turnaround bid. Austin and the board got essential legislative support and picked the right symbol—the campus makeover. Their strategy of linking UConn's ascendancy to the state's need to keep smart students in the state was brilliant.

Trustees in the first case, however, underestimated the legislature, and excluded those who would be most affected by their plan. They also seemed more intent on addressing the system's economic challenges than in meeting state needs.

SUMMARY

Ironically, by engaging university stakeholders in a series of discussions around strategic directions and values, the trustees in this case eventually redeemed themselves in the eyes of the public. Their new, more conventional, agenda enjoys reasonably broad support.

Dramatic turnarounds can and do occur in the public sector, as both the University of Connecticut and the College of New Jersey illustrate. The critical success factors that govern financial turnarounds generally described in chapter 2—savvy leadership, transparency, engagement of the faculty, and so forth—apply here as well. And while state treasuries cushion public institutions from financial catastrophe, state regulation, bureaucracy, and politics frequently hamstring them. To be successful in the public sector requires being liberated from the burden of excessive regulation—as occurred in both Connecticut and New Jersey—and attracting leaders who can link an institution's goals with a larger public agenda.

NOTES

1. David Osborne and Ted Gaebler, *Reinventing Government: How the Entrepreneurial Spirit is Transforming the Public Sector* (Reading, MA: Addison-Wesley, 1992).

2. Robert Birnbaum, *Management Fads in Higher Education: Where They Come From; What They Do; Why They Fail* (San Francisco: Jossey-Bass, 2000).

3. Robert Birnbaum, *How Academic Leadership Works: Understanding Success and Failure in the College Presidency* (San Francisco: Jossey-Bass, 1992).

4. Terrence MacTaggart and Associates, *Seeking Excellence Through Independence: Liberating Colleges and Universities from Excessive Regulation* (San Francisco: Jossey-Bass, 1998).

5. John Rawls, *A Theory of Justice*, rev. ed. (Cambridge, MA: The Belknap Press of Harvard University Press, 1999), 92.

6. James Martin and James E. Samels, *Merging Colleges for Mutual Growth: A New Strategy for Academic Managers* (Baltimore: The Johns Hopkins University Press, 1993).

7. Terrence J. MacTaggart and Associates, *Restructuring Higher Education: What Works and What Doesn't in Reorganizing Governing Systems* (San Francisco: Jossey-Bass, 1996).

8. Editorial, *Hartford Courant*, "Building Headaches at UConn," December 17, 2004, A12.

9. Fast Facts 2004, http:/www.uconn.edu/academicfacts.htm (retrieved October 5, 2006).

10. Darryl G. Greer, "Defining the Scope and Limits of Autonomy: New Jersey," in MacTaggart, *Seeking Excellence*, 84–106.

11. Robert O. Berdahl, "Balancing Self-Interest and Accountability: St. Mary's College of Maryland," in MacTaggart, *Seeking Excellence*, 59–83.

SECTION III

Lessons for Leaders

CHAPTER

Institutions in Distress—What Is a New President to Do?

Kenneth A. "Buzz" Shaw

Those of us who take on presidencies see ourselves as change agents; we earnestly believe that we can effectively lead our institutions to a higher level. I've never witnessed a new president saying that his goal was to keep the status quo, that his ambition was to avoid rocking the boat, and to enjoy a quiet 10 years. Generally, our egos wouldn't allow that, even if it were the best strategy. Neither are there many boards of trustees that would be interested in someone who presented herself or himself as the voice of mediocrity.

Most new presidents believe that their institutions will require change, but there are some campuses where transformative change will be necessary. This book deals with situations where there was need for more than simply tinkering around the margins: many of the institutions were clearly in distressed situations. By distress, I mean that the institution's very survival depended on wholesale, often radical change. That distress was usually financial, but often it involved leadership/governance issues and a general malaise that had turned ugly.

This chapter is written for the new president—not that there aren't presidents of long standing who are trying to exact a major turnaround. If in fact, however, an institution is in distress, it is usually time for its president to move on, as the trouble probably appeared on his or her watch. (That's not always true, of course, but is often the case.)

So, what is a new president to do? In this chapter, I will suggest activities that should precede taking the job, those that can occur after appointment but before the new person is installed, and those for the first two months on the job. Then, I will offer some specific suggestions for how to deal with the enormity of change that must take place.

BEFORE TAKING THE JOB

Woe betide the leader who thinks that an institution requires transforming change, but whose board and campus are quite happy, thank you, with the way things are. Woe, also, to the prospective president who sees a very good, stable place that will require change only on the margins, while the board and faculty see the situation as far more serious.

A prospective president must have a general sense of the situation before making any decision to engage in what could be a very meaningful and productive experience—or one that just doesn't work out. Thus, as a presidential candidate, you need to know and understand the situation, and know enough about yourself to ensure a good fit with that situation. Knowing one's self is an important part of emotional intelligence, one of the key characteristics of effective leaders. If you, the board, and the campus community have defined the need for transforming change, and if it is the challenge you have been craving, and if you see yourself as an effective change agent, then you can take the possible opportunity seriously.

If you are offered the position, and if you feel it is something you can and want to do, be certain that the board understands what is at stake for you. Members may have a good sense of what is at stake for the university, but they will likely have little understanding of what risks you are taking. One prospective president, when asked to take on a distressed institution, was quite candid with the board. "Look, I'm 55 years old. If I do what is needed here, and I am successful, you may have to get rid of me in five years. I may have burned out my candle. Even if I'm not burned out, the campus may no longer accept me as their leader because of what we've had to go through. So, I will need your understanding; I will also need the security of knowing that there is a place for me here. I don't want to be on the market for another presidency at age 60. I'm going to give my all to this one; if it doesn't work, I want the assurance of a tenured position, along with a salary commensurate to the contributions I've made and will make in my new role." If such situations are not agreed to in advance, chances are they won't be in the future, regardless of whether things go poorly or well. It is best to get such understandings in writing before you take on any presidency.

BEFORE TAKING OVER

Once you have negotiated an understanding about your future, you will usually have several months before you actually take over. That time should be effectively utilized. Of course, you will need to attend to the duties of your present position; however, you will find that things will likely quiet down—many problems and initiatives will be saved for whomever takes over your old job. So you can use the relative leisure to get ready.

Elsewhere, I suggest certain initiatives that presidential appointees can take before moving to their new offices.[1] Of course, as Michael Townsley reminds us in chapter 5, it's about the money, stupid. He describes the need to have "a sound financial management model that uses a set of accepted diagnostic, strategic, and reporting tools" to best ascertain the institution's financial condition.

You have every right to request such a model from your new business and financial offices. If your request is met with, "I want to be helpful but that isn't information we ordinarily keep," you already know you have a problem. But that is an opportunity for your vice president for business affairs to prove that she or he has what it takes to be on your team. An able administrator, even if it takes outside consulting, can develop the information for you in a format that you can understand. In fact, *insist* it be understandable! If it is not, make it the business officer's problem to make it such. (If your request is met with considerable resistance, you know you will need to act quickly to acquire a new business officer when you officially come on board.) Having that information will be very helpful. You might even want to speak directly with several of the people most versed in budget matters so you hear firsthand what the situation is.

Clearly, knowing the precise financial situation is essential, but there is much more you can do to ensure that you hit the ground running. Borrowing from my chapter in Robert Diamond's *Field Guide to Academic Leadership*, I suggest three strategies for your consideration:

- **Conduct a SWOT analysis.** Look at the institution's strengths, weaknesses, opportunities, and threats. You can ask senior-level administrators, deans, and select faculty and staff and student leaders to tell you what they think in writing—six pages or fewer, else you will get volumes. After reading that information, much will become apparent to you. Areas of agreement and disagreement about the challenges ahead will come into sharp focus. You will learn a great deal about the overall situation and will have some time to think about it before you arrive. The strategy is important: you won't have much time for reflective thought once you get on the job. You will also likely make allies of those you asked to become involved early on.

- **Consult with key board members.** The SWOT technique can also be modified to learn what board members are thinking. Talk with each of them individually about what they see the institution's strengths, weaknesses, opportunities, and threats to be. Be a good listener; you will learn a great deal. Your board will not only be pleased that you are taking charge, but that you are listening attentively to their views.

- **Consult with campus leaders.** Even though you won't be taking over for several months, there is nothing wrong with scheduling two- or three-day stints during the hiatus to visit with groups of faculty, students, and staff. Here, again, you are there to listen—to learn more about "our institution." You will be expected to say things, but for the most part people will understand that you don't have solutions to every problem at this point and time.

You should be feeling pretty good at that point: you're making an excellent start toward getting a handle on things. But the next two months will be critical.

Sixty Days to Set the Stage

In the Diamond chapter, I describe some early activities to get you started in the right way. Here are four of the best.

- **Walk around.** Take time to get to know your new people where they spend much of their time; they will be delighted by your attention, and you will learn a great deal. Walk around your new town; visit local cultural institutions; get to know restaurants and bookstores. Be visible, open, and positive. Always listen, and always show true appreciation and enthusiasm for the place you expect to call home for some time.

- **Talk with constituent leaders.** Learn who the constituent leaders are. Know what concerns they have. Now that you're the president, you can be specific in both your questions and your responses. Be sure they know how you plan to work with them. Setting your rules of engagement early on avoids ambiguity—and relationship mistakes.

- **Understand the governance system.** That will be essential. Your institution is in distress, but it does have a system of governance that defines how decisions are made. Be certain you understand it completely. If the system is not working, you need to know it well enough to make it better, as well as how use the right approaches to deal with the challenges ahead.

    You want to be sure to incorporate all those parts that do work into your planning. I've seen many presidents get into trouble because they neither understood nor respected their institution's governance system. Understanding and respecting it doesn't mean that you always go along with it. But if you don't understand it, procedural problems will plague you in your reform efforts.

    In other words, don't be like one new president who insisted on describing himself as his university's CEO. He refused to meet with groups whose goodwill he needed; instead, he directed his staff to carry out his orders. Not surprisingly, he lasted less than a year on the job.

- **Find the seams.** Those who play basketball, football, or other team sports know that the seam is the opening that can lead to a score. In our work, seams are the areas where change can happen most easily, the areas where campus governance or faculty involvement are not crucial to success. At one institution, for example, the student services operation was a seam. There was general overall dissatisfaction with the process, but faculty focused on other issues and left student services to the administration. Thus the new president was able to make a number of transforming changes without months of dialogue and debate. Of course, collaboration was required, but there was no need to involve the formal governance system. Frequently, distance education is a seam as well. Faculty members are generally involved in approving new programs, or sometimes new courses, but they leave it to their colleagues to determine the mode of delivery. It can be argued that distance education is just that: the same context, but a different method of delivery.

So far you have done well. People have appreciated your openness and your willingness to listen. They also see you as a quick study. But a couple of months have passed, and everyone is looking to see what happens next. "How will the new president lead us out of this situation?" "How will it affect me personally?" What follows are suggestions for your leadership role in these distressed times. Not all of them will work for you, but many will.

IT'S TIME TO LEAD

As MacTaggart suggests in chapter 1, different turnaround stages can require different leadership styles. He reminds us that an autocratic style is common for many financial turnarounds, but that it is often difficult for an autocratic leader to move an institution through a Stage III turnaround. He also describes the problem-solving leader as one adept at developing marketing and branding plans that help to tell an institution's story. Certainly institutions in distress need their leader to be a problem solver. But if an academic culture is to be redefined, if true transformation is to occur, the president must be a team leader, a person willing to collaborate with others.

Indeed, long-lasting, substantive change—true transformation—comes from leaders who not only inspire people with their vision, but are willing to listen to them and to work with them collaboratively to get things done. What follows are observations and suggestions to make you a true change-agent president.

- **Determine what the problems are and what strengths you can build on.** Too often leaders press for wholesale, transforming changes in all areas when some areas need only important, lasting change around their margins. Know what is needed and where. Do not follow the example of too many school superinten- dents in urban areas. A new person is appointed and then announces programs to cure all the ills of the school system. The basics of the new program usually comprise a catchy acronym that is forgotten when the leader flames out or moves to a bigger job just a few years later. To make a lasting impact, build on what is working first, and then focus on transformation in those areas that require it.

- **Understand the psychological environment.** Change is an emotional process. In *The Successful President: "Buzzwords" on Leadership*, I observe that universities and other social institutions go through a grieving process when they are dealing with major change, not unlike that attendant on the death of a loved one: denial, anger, bargaining, depression, and acceptance.[2] Don't forget that change is laden with heavy emotion; people are giving up the known for the unknown. To be suc- cessful, you can't ignore the very strong feelings that often accompany change.
  A new president once called to tell me that he just discovered his institu- tion was in serious financial difficulty. "No one told me," he said. He was, of course, hurt and angry about the surprise, even though it seemed his board was also unaware of how difficult the situation was. I said to him, "Would you have taken the job had you known the conditions?" He responded affirmatively. I then suggested that he move on—there was no real use in obsessing about what he should have known before; rather, he should focus his attention on acquir- ing a better understanding of what was needed. I reminded him of the stages of grieving and said that he would see them as he went through the transformative process. On numerous occasions during the next year he recounted to me how different groups were going through the stages. Finally, it appeared that most had reached the acceptance level. That new president learned to deal with the psychology of change.

- **Build a climate of trust.** Those leading change must be trusted. Robert House and his colleagues have conducted studies of leadership characteristics in 62 countries.[3] In all of them, trust was one of the prime attributes of effective leaders. When we think of trust, we, of course, think of people who are honest, honor their commitments, and are compassionate.

Throughout *The Leadership Challenge*, James Kouzes and Barry Posner emphasize the value of honesty. They point out that individuals don't want to be lied to, that they want their leaders to know right from wrong, and that they want the actions of their institutions to be ethical.[4] But trust also involves believing that our leaders know what they are doing—that they have the competence to lead us through change. Your new colleagues want to trust you as a person, and as someone qualified to lead them. That is why they brought you to your new institution.

- **Be transparent.** In chapter 2, MacTaggart reminds us of the importance of transparency. At Syracuse, when we went through financial restructuring, we opened our books to everyone. At that time, such action was unique for a private institution. Indeed, when the *New York Times* wrote an article about our financial difficulties, our disclosure gained national attention. Although many felt it would hurt our enrollment, it did not. And our openness gave us the creditability to move forward. Some had felt we had billions of dollars in reserves, and hence no problem. Showing our reserves silenced them. Others thought we were broke, and were headed for financial ruin. Our transparency helped people understand that was far from the case—that as a matter of fact we were poised to spend money to save money if it made sense (and it did, and we did).

- **Always focus on mission, vision, and core values.** Change doesn't come out of nowhere—it has to be grounded in what the institution represents. Franklin University, in Columbus, Ohio, has the same values today as when it was founded as a YMCA-affiliated institution "grounded in practical and applied studies" in 1902. They are: focusing on the mission, working for students, ensuring a quality academic product, serving its markets, building strategic relationships, supporting, encouraging, developing and recognizing its people, running like a business, and leading in education. While the mission has remained virtually the same, Franklin has continuously adapted to changing social conditions and to new approaches to pedagogy. Today, it annually enrolls nearly 10,000 students, a large majority of them working adults taking degrees at the associate, baccalaureate, and master's level. It has greatly expanded its online program and invested millions of dollars in curriculum development to ensure quality control. All of this occurred under the same set of values.

- **Walk the talk.** Be certain you're setting a good example yourself. For instance, it's not a good time to build a new presidential home, or even upgrade the presidential car. One president inherited a very expensive Cadillac from his predecessor. Although it had been a gift from a local dealer, it was a very obvious symbol to many. So one of his first moves was to buy a smaller car: comfortable and befitting the office, but not as ostentatious. The decision yielded much good publicity and showed his willingness to accommodate a leaner financial time.

- **Give people the tools to change.** Too often we misinterpret resistance to change as people being opposed to everything; in fact, people can deal with even enormous change if their fears are allayed and if they are given the reasons for change, as well as the tools and training to make those changes. At Syracuse, while we were cutting budgets, we spent millions of dollars on curriculum reform, quality improvement programs, and beefing up in-house development programs for staff. We said yes, we are a learning community, and yes, everyone is expected to learn. People were given the tools to change, making it easier for them to buy into the program.

One colleague gave this rationale for ensuring that all had the tools to change: Assume you start an assistant professor at $70,000 per year (obviously, salary norms vary by institution). If she earns tenure and stays for 30 years, when adjusted for small salary increases, just in salary alone the institution will have spent more than $3 million on her. How can we not give faculty and staff colleagues the tools to be successful, particularly when their institution is under great distress?

- **Use triage in dealing with resistance to change.** People's reactions to change take three forms: a willingness to support it once it is shown to be in their best interest, and in that of the institution; a desire to sit on the fence, and wait to see if it's going to take; and resistance regardless of value. Better to spend most of your time shoring up the committed and encouraging the fence-sitters. Trying to woo the strongly opposed diverts your energies and raises questions about your true commitment from those who would support you if you handled things correctly. Every institution has people in the third category; be polite, but don't let them occupy your time: others are watching.

    One president, for example, came to believe that if he could not get a particular faculty member to buy into a proposal, he would accomplish nothing. So the president focused on that individual, paying little attention to the fence-sitters, who might have yielded to persuasion. At the end of the day, the recalcitrant faculty member was not convinced; the fence-sitters stayed perched on the fence; and the original supporters of the change got tired of waiting. By becoming preoccupied with the wrong target, the president ignored those who could have helped him, and he failed to get his changes endorsed.

- **Persist.** In my experience and study of leadership, I've noticed that very little attention is given to persistence. We read and hear much about charisma, about transforming leaders, about the personal characteristics of leaders, about the environmental influences that affect what leaders can and cannot do, but little is said about what I believe is highly underrated and yet the most important trait in leading a turnaround—unfailing persistence.

    If you are persistent and can inspire others to be the same, it will not matter if you are not well-dressed or glib. Adhering unflinchingly to your goals outweighs superficial attributes. You want to be standing tall when your work is complete.

- **Respect your institution.** Over the years, your new institution has done many things right. Offer praise for that, while building on those things that are going well. Use the governance system as you work your way through the issues. Because early on you learned how it works, you have become a good mechanic, making it work during distressed times. You've also seen where initiatives had to be taken in other ways. Use alternate decision-making forms when needed, but explain why traditional processes were modified or supplanted.

    After Syracuse's restructuring plan was completed and announced in several open meetings to the university community, I was asked privately by a faculty colleague if I was planning to seek approval from the University Senate. I stated that I was not, because I felt that time was of the essence; we had involved literally hundreds of people—and many of the senate committees—in coming up with solutions, and it was time to move on. I did acknowledge, however, that any senator could put an issue on the agenda for discussion and vote. He said he thought he would do that, and I told him I understood. He did bring it up, and submitted a resolution that supported the plan; the senate voted unanimously to espouse it.

In other words, I had given the faculty the respect they deserved, and they reacted accordingly.

CONCLUSION

In most cases, you know what you are getting into when you accept an assignment to lead an institution in distress. I hope that my suggestions and advice will help you be successful in that endeavor. At the end of the day, it will be your skills, strengths, and persistence that will carry you and your institution through to success. Believe me, it will be worth all your efforts.

Good luck!

NOTES

1. Kenneth A. Shaw, "Creating Change: Suggestions for the New President," in *Field Guide to Academic Leadership*, ed. Robert M. Diamond (Hoboken, NJ: Jossey-Bass, 2002), 389–398.

2. Kenneth A. Shaw, *The Successful President: "Buzzwords" on Leadership* (Phoenix, AZ: ACE/Oryx Press, 1999).

3. Robert House, Paul J. Hanges, Mansour Javidan, and Peter W. Dorfman, eds., *Culture, Leadership and Organizations: The GLOBE Study of 62 Countries* (Thousand Oaks, CA: SAGE, 2004).

4. James Kouzes and Barry Posner, *The Leadership Challenge* (Hoboken, NJ: Jossey-Bass, 2002).

CHAPTER 8

Advice to Trustees, Donors, and Accreditors

Terrence MacTaggart

When asked why the trustees renewed the contract of an under-performing president at a struggling private college, the board chair responded, "This place probably couldn't attract someone much better in today's market." Problems at the college continued to mount, and following another budget crisis two years later, the board dismissed the president. That unfortunate delay not only deferred the beginning of a turnaround and allowed the college to get deeper in the hole, it required the trustees to offer a generous severance package that the college could ill afford. The only good news in the story is that the college did attract an experienced new leader, who has begun the turnaround process.

Versions of that story are surprisingly common at distressed colleges and universities. As mentioned in earlier chapters, it is often the faculty who capture the board's attention through a no-confidence vote in the president or other direct communications to the trustees. The supposed governors and stewards of an institution too often need to be prodded to deal with an incumbent leader's inability to address critical challenges.

This chapter offers practical advice to trustees and others, including donors and accrediting associations, on how to exercise their responsibilities toward struggling institutions. It suggests that those groups consciously tailor their actions to the relevant stage in the turnaround process. The chapter begins with advice to trustees on actions that should precede a turnaround—actions that may even make a turnaround unnecessary. It then recommends things that boards can do at each of the three stages in the turnaround process that will help make that phase more successful. It then offers some advice to trustees at public sector institutions. The chapter concludes with a shorter set of recommendations to donors and accreditors.

ANTICIPATING THE NEED FOR A TURNAROUND

Sometimes the need for a dramatic change in leadership and policies comes like a sudden bolt of lightning from a clear blue sky. But most of the time there are plenty of early warning signs of problems that trustees may choose to ignore and minimize—or act upon. It is understandable that trustees who know and like a president who assures them that better times lie just ahead will defer painful action. Any delay in dealing with serious problems, however, only worsens them.

Heed Early Warning Signs

Indicators of financial distress are hard to miss. Are enrollment and retention figures accurate? Do the numbers match projections, and are the projections sufficient to yield enough revenue to balance the budget? Are net assets growing or declining? Does the institution keep up with maintenance needs, or are the facilities deteriorating? Is there enough revenue to meet debt obligations? Are reserves adequate to handle unforeseen shortfalls? Is the endowment growing or shrinking in real terms?

The old saw that figures don't lie, but liars can figure applies to higher education. Trustees, working with their auditors, should certainly be alert to the possibility of theft and deception. However, especially for small institutions with a thin resource base, the problem is typically not fraud, but incompetence. Trustees should ask themselves if they really have confidence that the financial reports are accurate. They should meet with the external auditors—without the president and chief financial officer—for an unvarnished conversation about the reports, but also about the competence of financial managers and the worth of the systems on which they rely. Once the auditor leaves the room, trustees should ask themselves if they have reason to be confident in the auditor's competence and impartiality. To a nonfinancial executive, the ratios and analyses presented in chapter 5 may seem daunting. But any reasonably able senior financial officer should be adept enough to generate those numbers and explain them clearly to the board.

Of course, not all signs of distress show up in the budget. Prior to Buzz Shaw's arrival at Syracuse University, for example, the budget was balanced, and the university enjoyed adequate reserves. But to meet its financial objectives, Syracuse found itself dipping deeper and deeper into its applicant pool to fill the first-year class. Shaw's predecessor made the trustees aware of that insidious trend, and they acted to bring in a leader who could reverse it. Had the board members not heeded that clear early warning sign, the eventual turnaround would have taken longer and would have been more difficult to achieve.

Denial Is Not a River in Egypt

Outsiders are often astonished at a board's inaction in the face of explicit indicators that an institution is drifting, or plummeting, downward. But trustees are no more immune to the habit of denial than any other group where the politics of majority rule makes deferral a more comfortable choice than action.

Denial is simply a refusal to admit an unpleasant reality, an all too human wish to subscribe to the ostrich theory of problem solving. The following simple test will help trustees realize if they have unknowingly slipped into ignoring credible evidence. Answering four or five of the questions with a "yes" suggests a board is doing just that.

- Are the board members regularly told that some silver bullet—a new program, marketing effort, or generous donor—will soon resolve the major problems?
- Do the reasons alleged for failure almost always lie outside the control of the institution and its executives?
- Is the board told that current problems are just part of a down cycle or trend, and that patience alone is the answer to problems?
- Is a scapegoat on the board or within the institution regularly identified as the source of the problem, and is that used as an excuse for not solving it?
- In justifying the retention of the executive, do his or her champions point to past accomplishments, or loyalty, rather than current performance?

Why trustees often wait so long to take action is no mystery to anyone who knows how boards actually work. Alumni trustees often remain emotionally connected to the traditions they recall from their student days. They find even discussing the prospect of changing—going coeducational, dropping expensive sports teams, eliminating cherished academic programs—very painful. Factions within a board often offset one another, thus preventing decisive action, such as dismissing a president who is simply wrong for the times. Sometimes a board chair refuses to lead, especially if it means alienating others on the board or ending a close relationship with the executive. In those instances, other trustees must band together to take whatever actions are necessary to force the chair to act, or allow others to act.

Farewell and Hail

In our research, we found that no incumbent president who participated in the decline or allowed it to occur was able to launch a successful turnaround effort. A former vice president—like Jack Curry at Northeastern University—or another senior officer can rise to the position and the occasion to lead essential change, but an incumbent president apparently cannot. An old president has to go, and a new one must be selected—and supported—to produce a successful turnaround drama.

Dismissing a president should be done with respect, fairness, and dispatch. Fortunate are the boards that planned for the inevitable exit when their president entered. If the parties have already reached agreement on terms of transition, the exit process can be straightforward and amicable. Without a prior exit agreement, and assuming trustees choose not to seek dismissal for cause, however, the board will have to reach some settlement with the departing president. In those situations, trustees should seek to be fair to the individual and the institution. An overly generous exit package, especially if a president has not served for a long time and has failed to address the challenges, sends the wrong message to the campus community and adds to the school's financial woes.

In seeking and selecting a new leader who will turn around a college, trustees need to remember three important lessons illustrated in this book. First, while the immediate crisis may be financial, the turnaround will require marketing skills and, in all likelihood, some change in the academic culture as well. Thus a complete turnaround leader will possess the traits of a hardheaded financial manager but will also have a flair for marketing and academic reform, or the wisdom to hire people who can lead in those tasks. The most successful turnaround leaders are those who work effectively with others, including their own management team, as well as with faculty and other constituents.

Second, there is no substitute for a successful record of academic leadership. Dan Ritchie, who led the reversal in the fortunes of the University of Denver, is the exception in that he came from the corporate sector. His spectacular achievement should not overshadow the reality that the best candidate to lead a turnaround is most often someone who has done it at a college or university elsewhere.

Finally, trustees should realize that much of their new president's success depends on the board's commitment to the person and the task. Turnarounds are not a turnkey operation. They require trustees that are deeply and thoughtfully engaged in every phase of the strategy. Faculty, alumni, and community members may push back in the face of tough decisions necessary to a turnaround. Board members need to support their executive in those instances, so long as they are confident in the decisions he or she is making. In moving Northeastern to greater eminence as a research university, Richard Freeland needed to move faculty in the school's prized cooperative education program closer to the academic departments. He faced trenchant opposition from those in—and those allied to—the experiential learning programs. But in the end he enjoyed the unqualified support of the board; he prevailed, and Northeastern continues to move upward.

MATCH TRUSTEE LEARNING AND ACTION TO EACH TURNAROUND STAGE

Earlier in this book, we dissected common turnaround patterns into three stages. The financial makeover of the institution made up Stage I. Stage II focused on marketing and branding the institution and its signature programs. Revitalizing the academic core of the college or university by attracting and retaining better students, strengthening programs for them, and encouraging a better faculty represented Stage III. Not all institutions everywhere go through all three stages precisely in that order, but the model offers a useful template for understanding the turnaround process.

Chapter 2 further defined those stages and suggested a corresponding focus of trustee attention for each of them. Thus the stage of fiscal reform in the turnaround process requires intense exercise of the trustees' fiduciary responsibility. The board's duty to use its connections with figures important to the college—be they opinion leaders, potential donors, or politicians—is appropriate to the other-directed focus of Stage II. Finally, Stage III, with its attention to better students, better programs, and better faculty, requires that the board enlarge its strategic thinking to include the core of the institution, its entire educational effort.

This chapter borrows from the work of Richard Chait, William Ryan, and Barbara Taylor in delineating practical actions trustees can take at each stage of the turnaround process.[1] In all of the stages, the work of trustees will including learning about the stage at their institution; discussing with executives, other experts, and fellow trustees how the board can best contribute; and taking actions that will help the college move to a higher level of health and performance.

Stage I: Financial Reform

The essential trustee function in Stage I is fiduciary. For institutions with deficits and other indicators of financial distress, and those heading in that direction, here are some actions for trustees to take in consultation with the president and financial officers:

- Analyze operations to determine what is driving the downward-sloping fiscal trends
- Identify financial indicators that would signal a successful turnaround in finances or lack thereof
- Ensure that audit and finance committees are composed mainly of individuals with strong financial management experience
- Develop a job description for these committees that focuses on the demands of Stage I turnarounds
- Establish a strong relationship with the auditors and other external experts who can provide trustees with objective counsel on financial problems and turnaround strategies
- Report regularly and candidly to the entire board on the financial condition of the institution, steps taken to improve it, and the indicators to be used in evaluating progress in the turnaround
- Participate in the evaluation of the chief executive and senior financial officers in terms of their performance in leading the fiscal turnaround
- Evaluate annually the board's own performance in addressing the financial problems facing the college or university
- Systematically develop trustees' capacity to understand all aspects of financial turnarounds

Stage II: Marketing and Branding

The board's critical role during this phase of a turnaround is relational. Trustees need to understand the external relationships that are important to the institution's turnaround. They must appreciate the importance of designing and offering programs that meet market needs. They should study the strategies that contribute to an attractive reputation in the marketplace. "Brand," they must realize, is an asset of the institution that must be protected and enhanced, just as surely as buildings need to be maintained and laboratories and libraries updated. They should also learn where the college or university stands in relation to donors and potential donors, its capacity for fund-raising, and, in the case of public institutions, its relationship to the governor, legislature, and government regulatory agencies.

Trustees should consider actions such as the following to fulfill their Stage II responsibilities:

- Create committees—or reinvigorate moribund ones—whose chief responsibilities are marketing, development, and, for public institutions, government relations

- Ensure that committee members have substantial experience in those areas and that they appreciate the value of safeguarding and strengthening the institution's brand

- Cultivate the reputation of the board itself as credible, informed on key institutional matters, and committed only to the best long-term interests of the college, university, or system, along with those of the people it serves

- Protect the brand of the institution itself by ensuring that it fulfills its promises to its students and to the general public

- Develop benchmarks that measure progress in designing and vending programs that respond to market needs, that reflect improvements in the institution's image or reputation, and that chronicle fund-raising capacity and progress

- Acquire a practical understanding of the political and bureaucratic functions that deliver government support to the institution

- Develop a systematic approach to the board's role in private fund-raising, and insist that all trustees contribute not only individually, but to the larger advancement effort as well

- Nurture relationships with opinion leaders, politicians, and individuals with high net worth to advance the institution

- Evaluate their own performance in these areas, and take steps to improve their performance

- Report regularly to the board as a whole on success in marketing, branding, fund-raising, and, as appropriate, government relations

Stage III: Academic Revitalization

Because academic revitalization requires a complex set of activities in its own right, and because it affects the financial health of an institution, as well as how it is perceived by external audiences, Stage III demands the broadest strategic thinking from trustees. Stage III rests on the work of trustees in the preceding stages, alters the finances and the brand of the college or university, and, in large measure, determines the ultimate success of the institution as an educational enterprise.

Trustees have several choices for organizing themselves for such comprehensive work. An especially strong academic affairs committee, which also includes members with backgrounds in both finance and external relations, is one option. Another is to create a special strategic affairs committee to bridge those domains.

A third is to employ a committee of the whole with time set aside to study, discuss, and take appropriate actions that underpin academic renewal. Whatever the committee structure, work on Stage III will demand that the board take whatever time is necessary to discuss and understand the relationships between and among educational quality, finance, and brand. Reading Robert Morrill's superb text on trustee responsibility for academic leadership, *Strategic Leadership in Academic Affairs: Clarifying the Board's Responsibilities*, is a must at Stage III.[2]

The relationships between trustees and key institutional actors—faculty, students, and senior administrators, including the president—are distinctive and nuanced. In Stage I, trustees exercise substantial authority in assuring themselves, and other stakeholders, of the financial well-being of the institution. In Stage II they are more apt to act as equal partners with management in advancing the college or university. During the academic revitalization process, trustees sometimes behave as students in learning about the educational character of the place; sometimes as thoughtful experts on markets and public opinion, as they measure the potential for educational offerings; and, inevitably, as powerful stewards in assessing the costs of academic changes such as expanding programs or raising faculty salaries. Thus their roles will be participatory, consultative, or directive, depending on the issue at hand and on whether they are learning about an educational issue, discussing its merits, or deciding to approve its funding.

Specific actions for trustees approaching the complex work of Stage III change include:

- Organizing their committee structure, decision-making processes, and agenda setting set so that all members come to appreciate the connections between academic change and the aspects of trustee responsibility

- Developing, in conjunction with management, a clear sense of the roles of faculty, faculty governance bodies, the administration, and the trustees in the work of academic revitalization

- Scheduling the time, and structuring the conversations, that will enable trustees to understand the dynamics of Stage III change, as well as their multiple roles in it

- Consciously seeking learning opportunities that will give trustees a clearer intellectual understanding of the dimensions of academic renewal

- Engaging in experiential learning options, such as attending classes, enrolling in an online course, leading a seminar, or joining a field trip, that will provide a firsthand sense of the varieties of teaching-learning options available

- Becoming familiar with the available measures of educational effectiveness that are relevant to the institution they govern

ADVICE TO PUBLIC UNIVERSITY TRUSTEES

In *Good to Great*, Jim Collins identifies the factors that distinguish merely successful companies from the truly great ones. He reports that he offended nearly everyone in a room of corporate CEOs when he rejected the idea that the way for a nonprofit to become great was to "act more like a business."[3] Collins goes on to say, "We need to reject the naïve imposition of 'the language of business' on the social sectors, and instead jointly embrace a *language of greatness*" (emphasis in original).[4]

In some respects, of course, colleges and universities do resemble businesses, and should seek all the efficiencies demanded of for-profit enterprises. They need to control costs and increase revenues. They charge a price (tuition and fees) for a service (education) delivered by a workforce (faculty and staff) at physical locations (campuses), using many kinds of technology (from blackboards to computers). With the important exception of proprietary schools, however, their purpose is to deliver education, research, and service, not to make a profit. Colleges and universities are often branded based on how much they acquire, and how much they spend on students, not on how efficient they are at delivering well-prepared graduates. And authority is more diffuse at colleges and universities than in any imaginable corporation. If the governance gap is wide between all higher education and the corporate sector, it is gargantuan when it comes to publicly subsidized state colleges and universities.

Trustees who come to their governing roles with more experience in the corporate than the public sector would do well to remember those constants for trusteeship at public institutions. To ignore these facts of life is the rough equivalent of deciding to do business in China while insisting that cultural differences don't matter.

Governance Takes Place in the Sunshine

Trustees need to know and abide by their state's open meeting and open record laws. Trying to circumvent them creates the appearance that a board has something to hide, and throws subsequent work of the board under a cloud of suspicion. In reality, a reporter's presence is usually less of a problem than some trustees fear. Most journalists are objective in their reporting, and many develop a helpful sympathy for the institution they cover. Trying to dodge the very few ornery investigative journalists only makes matters worse.

Trustees should not expect legislative relief from open meeting rules anytime soon. Attempts to change laws to darken sunshine requirements have been uniformly unsuccessful. Legislators, like journalists, prefer the work of trustees to be in the open.

Such constraints may be in stark contrast to corporate governance (although increased transparency there is now also a matter of law) and to that of private colleges and universities. But at state-supported schools, the public's right to know trumps an institution's desire for privacy. As the case of the troubled system presented in chapter 6 demonstrates, trying to keep important plans and strategies a secret usually makes implementing them impossible.

Political Involvement Is the Rule, Not the Exception

Public colleges and universities are immersed in a political environment. Their boards of trustees are typically appointed and confirmed by popularly elected governors and legislators. Some boards, such as those in Michigan, Nevada, and

Nebraska, are themselves elected. And while the percentage of state support for public colleges may be declining relative to their total budgets, those monies are still essential to the operations of most. It is extremely naïve, even irresponsible, for trustees to ignore the fact that financial support is allocated through a political process of deliberation and compromise.

Successful turnarounds in the public sector demand that trustees embrace the opportunities and manage the constraints imposed by their political environment. Instead of merely coping with the legislature, trustees need to nurture champions within it, and, if they cannot convert critics into supporters, at least neutralize them. The transformation of the University of Connecticut into a premier public research university is being accomplished in part by brilliant orchestration of its relations with the governor and the legislature.

The Academic Agenda Must Match the Public's Agenda

It's still about the economy. Providing the people of a state with access to the education they need to compete, performing research that addresses current economic and social needs, and directly supporting business and economic development are all ways of aligning the academic agenda with the public agenda.

As the unsuccessful attempt to merge campuses described in chapter 6 illustrates, the members of the public must not view change as an *administrative* priority of the trustees, but as a *public* priority. By contrast, one of the reasons UConn's rise in the ranks of public research universities is so successful is because its aims are widely viewed as solidly aligned with the goals of the state. By reversing the outflow of talented students and by otherwise serving needs that citizens value, the university has integrated its agenda for excellence with the public's desires. The notion that the citizens of New Jersey deserved a state-supported institution that approached Princeton in quality, but not cost, defined the transformation of Trenton State to The College of New Jersey.

ADVICE TO DONORS AND ACCREDITORS

"We're invisible," one president of a small, struggling college complained in describing donors' aversion to supporting those kinds of institutions. "We're the ones who give society's disenfranchised a chance to get a degree and a better life," he continued, "but the money goes to the Harvards that, frankly, don't need it." In the same seminar, supported by the Davis Educational Foundation, another president at a similar college accused her accrediting association of scrutinizing the smaller, less prestigious schools, while giving a pass to the larger, more established institutions. Rodney Dangerfield would feel at home with those beleaguered executives.

But it is true that donors and regulatory agencies often treat distressed institutions differently than those with solid financial and enrollment bases. And they should. Philanthropies have a fiduciary responsibility to *their* donors to make grants and donations prudently. That often means supporting safe institutions rather than those that run the risk of becoming lost causes. Accrediting associations, along with state and federal approval authorities, have a responsibility to protect consumers. Accrediting groups in particular seek to balance their goals of improving institutional performance with safeguarding students from marginal academic programs, hyperbolic promises of postgraduate employment, and fly-by-night operations that may not be in business next week.

But those groups can also do a better job of fulfilling their own duty to funders, taxpayers, and the public, while still helping struggling colleges become stronger. To do so, they need to tailor their policies and actions to the appropriate turnaround stage. Sometimes that will include forcing a college's board and executive to actually jump-start a turnaround.

Donors

At a critical point in his financial makeover of Green Mountain College, President Jack Brennan secured a $750,000 gift from a generous donor. The money had no strings attached, allowing Brennan to apply it to where it was needed most—and he had no shortage of needs. The timing, amount, and flexible character of the gift perfectly matched the turnaround point of the college. Selfless donors will recognize that during the first stage of a turnaround it is more important to give largely unrestricted cash than to insist the money go for something more important to the donor than to the college.

Early in the evolution of Syracuse University from a traditional research university to one centered on students, Chancellor Buzz Shaw persuaded a donor to contribute five million dollars to develop Meredith Professors. That award provided a significant salary supplement, plus professional expense money, to research scholars who were also excellent teachers. Again, timing the donation to the most important need helped propel Syracuse's particular transformation.

By focusing gifts on what an institution needs most to accelerate its turnaround—not necessarily what a donor might prefer—philanthropists can magnify the benefits of their gift. In the early days of a Stage I financial change, unrestricted cash is often the most important resource, and the hardest to realize from college revenues alone. Capacity building, as in the Syracuse example of Meredith Professors, makes sense in Stages II and III. Contributions to endowed professorships, laboratory and library renewal, and new or enhanced academic programs, such as the gifts of Ray and Carole Neag to cancer research and the School of Education at the University of Connecticut, are well timed to speed academic revitalization. If the trustees' goal is to build a stronger institution, their mantra at each point in the turnaround trajectory should be "let the gift match the need."

Accreditors

Simply put, accrediting associations will help struggling colleges to right themselves if they offer more tough love than if they permit those schools to avoid decisive action. One religiously affiliated college received warnings year after year but failed to improve its finances until asked to show cause why it should not lose accreditation. Then, in quick order, the leaders of the denomination found a capable president, committed the necessary funds, and otherwise assured the accrediting group that progress would be made. The real turnaround had begun.

Like donors, accrediting associations need to match their attention to the transformational stages. Schools in the midst of Stage I financial turnarounds, and those that ought to be, are best served by accrediting review teams that comprise tough-minded financial officers and financial aid experts who will ensure that no one is cutting corners for the sake of dollars. When schools are hotly engaged in developing and marketing new programs, review teams and commissions need to emphasize their standards for integrity and academic quality. In those Stage II situations, an institution must be held to high expectations for truth in advertising. For those colleges that have found their way financially and have achieved a reliable flow of students for their programs, accrediting groups can encourage a focus on academic revitalization. The appropriate role for accreditation in Stage III change is a consultative one that encourages peer academics to exercise thoughtful creativity in strengthening educational programs and environments.

Boards of trustees deserve greater attention from the accrediting groups than they currently receive. As mentioned often in this book, the supposed ultimate guardians of institutional health too often ignore or downplay early warning signs of distress, or believe that their work on a turnaround is done once they hire a new executive. A liberal arts college that is merrily burning through its endowment without a credible plan to reverse its downward trend does so because its board is not doing its job. Accrediting groups would serve that institution, and others like it, much more effectively if they included able trustees on their teams, insisted that board chairs attend meetings where institutional performance is reviewed, and denied accreditation to schools where the board failed in its stewardship.

SUMMARY

Trustees are ultimately responsible for the well-being of the institution they oversee. When a college has slipped, they need to find, and collaborate with, the right executive to put it back on track. But trustees are helped mightily by donors who provide the right gifts at the right time and by accreditors and state overseers who insist an institution face its problems.

NOTES

1. Richard Chait, William Ryan, and Barbara Taylor, *Governance as Leadership: Reframing the Work of Nonprofit Boards* (Hoboken, NJ: John Wiley & Sons, 2004).

2. Richard Morrill, *Strategic Leadership in Academic Affairs: Clarifying the Board's Responsibilities* (Washington, DC: Association of Governing Boards, 2002).

3. Jim Collins, *Good to Great and the Social Sectors* (self-published monograph, 2005), 1.

4. Ibid., 2.

INDEX

ABOUT THE
CONTRIBUTORS

Terrence MacTaggart is the principal author of this volume. Jerry Berberet, Adrian Tinsley, and Michael Townsley wrote individual chapters on their areas of expertise, while Buzz Shaw offers advice to new presidents. Tom Longin and Charles Cook contributed significantly to the thinking about turnarounds presented here and to some of the research on specific turnaround institutions.

TERRENCE MACTAGGART has conceptualized and edited two books on governance and transformation at public institutions: *Restructuring Higher Education: What Works and What Doesn't in Reorganizing Governing Systems*, and *Seeking Excellence Through Independence: Liberating Colleges and Universities from Excessive Regulation*, both published by Jossey-Bass. He has also led institutional turnarounds. While chancellor at the University of Wisconsin–Superior from 1987 to 1991, he orchestrated a revitalization effort that resulted in improved state funding, growth in enrollment, and in The Superior Plan, an academic reform effort.

As head of the University of Maine System from 1996 to 2001, he was responsible for increased state funding for higher education, and he developed a governance model known as "entrepreneurial universities-efficient systems." During that period, he led several successful statewide efforts to secure voter approval to make more capital investment in Maine's public universities. In 2006, the trustees of the University of Maine System asked him to again serve as chancellor for a one-year term to focus on further improving state support.

MacTaggart also serves as a consultant to trustees and presidents of public and independent institutions on topics of governance and strategic improvement.

JERRY BERBERET served as the founding executive director of the Associated New American Colleges (ANAC) from 1995 to 2006. Prior to that he was a founding member of a study group of chief academic officers that organized in 1990 to analyze the essential identity and differentiating characteristics of small to midsize private comprehensive colleges and universities, an inquiry that led to creation of

ANAC. Earlier, he was an associate professor of history and director of environmental science at SUNY–Plattsburgh; dean of liberal arts at Willamette University, in Oregon; and vice president for academic affairs at North Central College, in Illinois. He has collaborated with the Carnegie Foundation for the Advancement of Teaching, the University of North Carolina, and the University of Minnesota in national surveys of the professoriate at various stages of faculty careers. His most recent book (with Linda McMillin) is *A New Academic Compact: Revisioning the Relationship between Faculty and Their Institutions*, published by Anker Publishing Company in 2002. He holds a PhD in American history.

CHARLES COOK served for 24 years as the director of the Commission on Institutions of Higher Education, which accredits all private and public colleges and universities in the six New England states. Currently he is senior vice president for university affairs for Johnson & Wales University, where his portfolio includes strengthening both institution-wide governance and quality assurance. He is a trustee of Lesley University, in Cambridge, Massachusetts, and the American College of Greece, in Athens. Cook has taught as an adjunct instructor at the University of Maryland, DePaul University, and Harvard University.

TOM LONGIN, formerly chief academic officer at Seattle University and Ithaca College, and recently retired vice president at the Association of Governing Boards of Colleges and Universities, has an intimate knowledge of the roles of presidents and trustees in leading turnarounds. He has done board workshops and professional presentations on the respon-sibilities of governing boards, institutional governance, the board and institutional plan-ning, and strategic leadership in academic affairs. Longin has also authored an extended essay, "Institutional Governance: A Call for Collaborative Decision-Making," in *The New Academic Compact: Revisioning the Relationship between Faculty and Their Institutions*, pub-lished by Anker Publishing Company in 2002, and frequently consults with independent institutions on the leadership responsibilities of trustees, presidential selection, governance and academic affairs, and governance and strategic planning.

KENNETH A. "BUZZ" SHAW is the former chancellor of Syracuse University and was previously president of the University of Wisconsin System. He has also served as chancel-lor of the Southern Illinois University System, president of Southern Illinois University at Edwardsville, and vice president and dean of Towson University, in Maryland.

At Syracuse, Shaw directed an extensive restructuring process and initiated the transfor-mational change that led Syracuse to redefine itself as a leading student-centered research university. He is a former chair of the board of trustees of the Commission on Indepen-dent Colleges and Universities and a member of the board of directors of the American Council on Education. His most recent books are *The Successful President: "Buzzwords" on Leadership*, published by the American Council on Education/Oryx Press, and *Intentional Leadership*, published by Syracuse University Press.

ADRIAN TINSLEY led a turnaround in funding, facilities, and academic programs during her 13 years as president of Bridgewater State College, in Massachusetts. Since leaving the presidency in June 2002, Tinsley has served as a visiting scholar with the Harvard Graduate School of Education and as "president-in-residence" for Harvard's master's degree program in higher education. She has also taught a leadership seminar at the University of Massachusetts–Boston. Tinsley is a founding faculty member of the Bryn Mawr Institute for Women in Higher Education, held every summer at Bryn Mawr College since 1975.

MICHAEL T. TOWNSLEY, formerly president of the Pennsylvania Institute of Technology and senior vice president for finance and administration at Wilmington College, is currently a professor of business at Becker College. in Worcester, Massachusetts. He also consults widely with independent colleges on financial management and strategy. He is the author of *The Financial Toolbox for Colleges and Universities* and *The Small College Guide to Financial Heath: Beating the Odds,* both published by the National Association of College and University Business Officers.